# THEMES
and
# VARIATIONS
for a
# CHRISTIAN
# DOXOLOGY

# Themes and Variations for a Christian Doxology

*Being*

## The Clinton Lectures

*Delivered Spring Semester, 1989*
*University of Dubuque Theological Seminary*
*Dubuque, Iowa*

*by*

## Hughes Oliphant Old

WILLIAM B. EERDMANS PUBLISHING COMPANY
GRAND RAPIDS, MICHIGAN

Copyright © 1992 by Wm. B. Eerdmans Publishing Co.
255 Jefferson Ave. S.E., Grand Rapids, Michigan 49503

Printed in the United States of America

**Library of Congress Cataloging-in-Publication Data**

Old, Hughes Oliphant.
Themes and variations for a Christian doxology: being the Clinton
lectures, delivered spring semester, 1989, University of Dubuque
Theological Seminary, Dubuque, Iowa / by Hughes Oliphant Old.
p.      cm.
ISBN 0-8028-0614-7 (paper)
1. Public worship.   I. Title.   II. Title: Clinton lectures.
BV15.045   1992
264'.001 — dc20                              92-24691
                                                      CIP

Unless otherwise noted, the Scripture quotations in this publication are
from the Revised Standard Version of the Bible, copyrighted 1946, 1952
© 1971, 1973 by the Division of Christian Education of the National
Council of Churches of Christ in the U.S.A., and used by permission.

*To Arlo D. Duba*

# Contents

# Preface

The invitation to be Clinton Visiting Professor for the spring semester of 1989 at the University of Dubuque Theological Seminary gave me the incentive to sit down and try to think out a simple, clear, and basic theology of worship, something of interest to serious theological students whose primary aim was to go out into the pastorate and lead the people of God in Christian worship. Dubuque seemed like the sort of place I would find that kind of student, and indeed I did.

When I got there, I found the students were ready to take me on. Things got off to a great start when Dallas Walker came to my room and told me what he was expecting. He was not about to put up with a lot of academic pretentiousness, but if I was willing to put all that aside he could be very interested in the subject. It soon became clear that he was the class nonconformist. He had been in the Navy a number of years and was heading back to the chaplaincy. I sensed there were some real questions there and decided I wanted to take them as earnestly as they had been posed.

Rick Pfeil was a graduate of Oral Roberts University who had had several years of experience as a youth worker at a Presbyterian church in Pennsylvania before deciding to come to seminary. He was a careful and exacting student with a solid knowledge of Scripture. From him I learned that thoroughly explaining the passages of Scripture from which I was getting all this did indeed get across the point.

My California evangelicals, Dave Zazvorka and Tom Patterson, gave me much the same reading. They sat in the back row following in their Bibles and smiling. Besides that they wrote very good examination papers. When Tom graduated, he received a call to a congregation of Native Alaskans on an island near Ketchikan. He and his wife had already spent a year up there on an internship, so he was quite realistic about what he was going to have to do. I found myself very much wanting to teach something that would be useful for him.

Then there was Sally Hart, an organist in a Dutch Reformed congregation out in the middle of Iowa. When I discovered how serious she was about the ministry of praise and it became obvious what an excellent student she was, I began including all kinds of material with her in mind.

It was the same way with Bill Barrett. Regrettably the class was scheduled for 7:30 in the morning, and although he was in all other points a good Methodist, he was not very Wesleyan in the matter of rising early in the morning. What I got across to Bill was done in the coffee shop at lunchtime. He was a voracious reader and took Karl Barth as gospel. I included quite a bit of material for him as well but, alas, when I had an especially juicy quotation from Charles Wesley or Karl the Great, Bill's alarm clock failed to achieve its purpose. Well, that is all right, I suppose. He did seem to do quite a bit of reading for the course. I have to admit that most of my education was gotten in the library rather than in the classroom. Besides, I rather enjoyed having coffee with him and arguing theology. With the publication of these lectures he may finally find out what I had to say.

Ben Ray, the son of a Presbyterian minister from Kansas, was another one who elicited from me information I might not otherwise have included. He was very proud of his Italian heritage. He looked Italian, too — tall, dark wavy hair, and soulful brown eyes. He was as committed to the preaching ministry as his father before him, and for that reason alone I am sure he will be a very fine pastor. I wanted to tell him about the fifteenth-century Italian preachers I so much admired. That is part of his heritage too! I will never forget the spring evening he took me to Mario's for pasta and Italian pastry.

My very enjoyable semester was almost over when the First Presbyterian Church of Clinton, Iowa, which each year underwrites the Clinton Lectures, invited me for dinner. All the plenty of the Midwest was spread out carry-in dish style. They wanted to hear what I had done for the semester. I had taken Tom Patterson and Cathy Young with me to talk about the ministry they intended to exercise and how the Clinton lectureship and the seminary course of study in general would help them in their work. Tom told about the church in Alaska he intended to serve, and Cathy Young told about her plans. She was (and, I presume, still is) a housewife in a prosperous Iowa town where her husband owns his own business, and the ministry she plans to exercise is in her hometown. She is a sensible, intelligent woman who certainly communicated to all of us that night the value of a solid theological education to the grass roots of the American church.

When acknowledgments are to be made, it is certainly to such people that expressions of thanks are due. They helped write the book, and it is for them, and people like them, that the book is written.

Trenton, New Jersey
April 1991

# I

## Doxology as the Theology of Worship

There have been several notable attempts in the last few years to write a liturgical theology or, even more simply, a theology of worship. In fact, ever since the middle of our century, the study of liturgy has begun to emerge as a distinct branch of the theological sciences. With the impressive mass of historical data that has been collected on this subject in the last generation, it is hardly surprising that now there are those who are beginning to ask what the theology of worship might be. Surely among the past decade's most impressive attempts to write a theology of worship is Geoffrey Wainwright's *Doxology*. One thinks of David Noel Power's *Unsearchable Riches* and Aidan Kavanagh's *On Liturgical Theology* as well.[1] It seems to me that Wainwright has given us the right name for this rapidly developing field of theology — that is, *doxology*.

---

1. Geoffrey Wainwright, *Doxology: The Praise of God in Worship, Doctrine, and Life* (New York: Oxford University Press, 1980); David N. Power, *Unsearchable Riches: The Symbolic Nature of Liturgy* (New York: Pueblo Publishing, 1984); Aidan Kavanagh, *On Liturgical Theology* (New York: Pueblo Publishing, 1984). Of particular interest is the discussion by these three theologians of each other's works: Power on Wainwright, *Worship* 55 (1981): 61-69; Wainwright's reply to Power, *Worship* 55 (1981): 448-51; Wainwright on Kavanagh, *Worship* 61 (1987): 183-86; and Kavanagh on Wainwright, *On Liturgical Theology*, pp. 123-25.

1

The name doxology commends itself because it presses us to go beyond mere cultic acts and rituals and to see all these things in terms of the serving of God's glory. Even more, Wainwright has so very clearly related Christian worship, Christian thought, and Christian action.

# I

More than one of us has wondered just what it is we are supposed to be doing when we come together on Sunday morning. It has often been a significant experience when we have been lifted up by an inspiring sermon, deeply moved when the congregation has sung well-loved hymns with enthusiasm, and aware of God's presence when the Lord's Supper has been celebrated with high seriousness. Most of us have had those wonderful experiences at a summer conference when vespers has been held out in the woods or looking out over a lake at sunset when there was a reverent hush and no one had to explain what was going on. One perhaps does not have to explain to a mother why she prays with her child at bedtime. And yet one does wonder what worship is. One wonders what it is that makes it so sacred to say a blessing at a family meal, the simplest of all acts of worship. Sometimes we do it in such a perfunctory way, and we ask ourselves what the point of it is. The question of what worship really is becomes particularly troublesome when we sense that something is not quite right about it, when only a discouragingly small congregation shows up, when the minister drones on about the woes of the world, and the organist drags out hymns that no one sings. It seems like such an effort. We ask ourselves whether it is worthwhile keeping it all up. On the other hand, we may find ourselves asking the question when we are in some splendid gothic church for Christmas Eve vespers and the service of worship has been turned into a concert. There are crowds of people there, but one asks what they are all there *for*. There is not even a final benediction. With a certain annoyance one asks what worship is supposed to be.

Participation in lame, hollow, or misdirected worship may well make for an agonized posing of the question as to the true nature of worship, but it is the awareness of true worship that makes our questioning bear the fruit of understanding. It is because "a day in thy courts is better than a thousand elsewhere" that we again and again come to worship. So many of us have had the experience of going from strength to strength as we have followed the highways to Zion. And when all is said, generation after generation the church has been firm in the affirmation of the Psalmist, "How lovely is thy dwelling place, O LORD of hosts!" (84:1). Yes, in spite of the shortcomings it often has, many of us "feel good about" worship, to use the parlance of our day, and for some that is sufficient reason to worship. For others of us it is important to press the question further.

There is something objective about worship that makes it more real than our feelings about it. Whether our worship has been the worship that is in spirit and truth is not really determined by our subjective feelings. Any minister ought to know that. We preach a sermon that for some reason just does not seem to get off the ground, and then later we find someone for whom it was a word of hope. Evidently more was going on than we had felt was going on. One does not have to be a minister to have the experience of praying long and sincerely over some problem and then one day, after despairing of our prayer's being heard, discovering all of a sudden that it was heard, and answered in a way we never expected. It is the same way with our praise. It may seem to languish because times are tough and even God's people are discouraged, yet when joined to the praise of angels and archangels it may indeed become a mighty hallelujah chorus. That was the way it was revealed to John on the island of Patmos one Lord's

3

Day. By revelation he discovered that there was an eternal dimension to his lonely worship.

Worship, we would like to maintain, has dimensions to it that neither art nor entertainment have. And, strangely enough, this is often lost sight of by those who devote themselves to the cultivation of the liturgy. How enjoyable a service of worship may or may not be is not the ultimate question in the evaluation of worship. Whether we ask about this enjoyment from a more popular standpoint or from a more discriminating and more aesthetic standpoint, we must be careful to recognize that something very different is going on in worship than in a Philadelphia Symphony Orchestra concert or a Broadway show. The best liturgical texts are rarely great literature. While the Scottish Psalter is hardly great poetry, even Robert Burns testified to its surpassing value as worship. In "The Cotter's Saturday Night," Burns tells of the evening prayers in the home of a humble Scottish family. When he speaks of singing "those strains that once did sweet in Zion glide," what he has in mind, of course, is the singing of the Scottish Psalter.

> They chant their artless notes in simple guise;
>     They tune their hearts, by far the noblest aim:
> Perhaps Dundee's wild warbling measures rise,
>     or plaintive Martyrs, worthy of the name;
> Or noble Elgin beats the heav'nward flame,
>     The sweetest far of Scotia's holy lays.

The greatest poets have not always been the best hymnodists. And the contrary is true as well. There are many hymns that have been greatly beloved and have served the glory of God for generations that no one would claim as great poetry. Paul Gerhardt, Isaac Watts, and Charles Wesley rank among the greatest hymnodists, but, quite properly, no one confuses them with the leading poets of their centuries. This is not to say that we cannot identify many poetic qualities in the classic hymns of the church but simply that poetry and hymnody are not quite the same thing. There is a dimension to hymnody that mere poetry does not have. That is why we ask about doxology, the theology of worship.

Surely there is a place for delighting in worship. Even the Puritans were glad to say that man's chief end is to glorify God *and to enjoy* him forever. So many of the Puritans tell us of their surpassing delight in worship. One of the first theological works written in America, Thomas Shepard's *Wise and Foolish Virgins,* is filled with this sense of delighting in prayer and praise.[2] No one could be more eloquent on this subject than Jonathan Edwards. In his *Faithful Narrative* he tells us of how the Great Awakening brought his congregation to a deeper appreciation of worship.[3] They feasted on preaching, they rejoiced in psalmody, and they flocked to the Lord's Table with sacred joy. As Edwards saw it, the children of God delight in the things of God. They rejoice in being edified by the preaching of the Word. It refreshes and illumines them, and in this they find delight. There is no greater happiness than to be in communion with God, and the celebration of the Lord's Supper is the feast day of this communion. As Edwards saw it, it is the religious affections that draw us to Christ and transform us into his likeness.[4] The ordinances of worship, the disciplines of prayer, the exercise of praise, the reading and preaching of Scripture, and the celebration of the sacraments are the means God has appointed for nurturing these religious affections. This is how the Holy Spirit works in our

2. Shepard's *Parable of the Wise and Foolish Virgins* was first published in London in 1659. It is included in the complete works of Thomas Shepard, which were published in Boston in 1857. An AMS reprint of this edition is currently available.

3. Jonathan Edwards, *A Faithful Narrative,* in vol. 4 of *The Works of Jonathan Edwards* (New Haven: Yale University Press, 1972).

4. See Edwards, *The Religious Affections,* in vol. 2 of *The Works of Jonathan Edwards* (New Haven: Yale University Press, 1959).

hearts and minds. When this happens and we sense that it is happening, there is a holy delight in worship. Edwards would insist that worshiping God is a means of both glorifying God and enjoying him forever. That is to say, the delight is not so much in the worshiping as in the one who is worshiped. It is, in the end, God who is delightful. When we find our delight in him, then God is worshiped.

Still there is the question of what it is we are supposed to be doing when we come together for worship. Just what is the service we are to render in our preaching, in our praises, our prayers, and our celebration of the sacraments? That is why we ask about the theology of worship. What is the sense of doing this which we do?

There have always been those who have sought to locate the significance of worship in what it has done for people. Worship must be a service. Is it not, after all, called the *service* of worship? Should the service of worship, then, not do some sort of good to those who attend? One can always make the point that indeed it does. Worship, some would explain, provides moral instruction that makes for better citizens and therefore a better society. One does not even have to believe in God to advance this argument. There has been no end of politicians whose religious commitments were only marginal but who supported religion for its social benefits. This approach was particularly characteristic of the Enlightenment. The only thing such people seemed to be interested in was whether worship produced better morals among the common people. Others like to consider the social value of the sacraments. As rites of passage, they help people fit into the community. Baptism helps us adjust to the responsibilities of parenthood and expresses to us the support of the community when a new child is born. Confirmation helps teenagers to make the transition from childhood to adulthood. Marriage makes an official beginning for a new family. Communion becomes a way of extending social acceptability to each member of the society. And funerals give us an opportunity to make a final separation with a friend or member of the family. Here, again, one does not really have to believe in God to defend religious rites with this argument. One would not want to deny certain social benefits to the celebration of worship, but that is not why we worship God. There is nothing wrong with asking about the social benefits of worship, but that is not the question we want to ask here.

To be sure, worship is a service, but it is a service to God. In the German language the word most commonly used for worship is *Gottesdienst* — that is, "the service of God." *Gottesdienst* is very closely related to *Menchendienst,* "service to man," but there is an obvious distinction. The service of man does not necessarily go hand in hand with the service of God, nor does the service of God always entail the service of the neighbor, although Jesus wanted to make the point that if service of God is the first commandment, then the service of the neighbor is the second and is very much "like unto it." From a Christian standpoint, true service of God is the root of the most consequential service of the neighbor. The service of man flows from the service of God. Without a genuine service of the neighbor, there is no real service of God. Without love, the apostle Paul tells us, any kind of religious service is but a clanging gong and a tinkling cymbal. Yet, on the other hand, naked social service, without religious devotion, is just as false. It ends up being *Göttzendienst,* "the service of idols." There is a great deal of idolatry involved in the various social, political, and economic ideologies of modern secular states. The idolatries of the French Revolution, Nazi Germany, and Communist Russia are only the most obvious. The modern church can become quite as idolatrous as the modern state if she begins to figure that social service is all that really matters, puts all her energies into what she thinks is Christian social service, and neglects the service of worship.

John Calvin spoke to this issue very clearly in his commentary on the book of Micah. He reminds us that Christian service has to do with the second table of the Law, while worship has to do with the first. The first and greatest commandment is to love God, and the *second* is to love the neighbor.[5] Gilbert Tennent, preaching in Philadelphia a generation before the American Revolution, delivered several sermons on the serving of God's glory in which he proclaimed that it is above all in the service of worship that we bring to God the love that Jesus calls for in the first and greatest commandment.[6] What I would like to do, then, in the pages that lie before us, is to throw some light on the question of how our worship serves God's glory.

## II

One question we must ask before we can enter into a discussion of the significance of our worship is how we are to look for it. Where is it that we go to ask these questions about the meaning of our service of worship? The ultimate place in which we must search for the meaning of our worship is in God's calling us to live to the praise of his glory, his creating us to serve him. The apostle Paul, perhaps better than anyone else, put his finger on it when he taught that out of God's love

5. For a discussion of this passage as well as this whole dimension of Calvin's theology of worship, see my article "John Calvin and the Prophetic Criticism of Worship," in *John Calvin and the Church: A Prism of Reform,* ed. Timothy George (Louisville: Westminster/John Knox Press, 1990).

6. In 1744 Gilbert Tennent published a series of sermons on the Westminster Shorter Catechism, *Twenty-three Sermons upon the Chief End of Man, the Divine Authority of the Sacred Scriptures, the Being and Attributes of God and the Doctrine of the Trinity.* The following year a second volume appeared, *Several Discourses on Important Subjects.* The two volumes are in effect an attempt at a systematic theology, though it was never completed.

for us in Christ we "have been destined and appointed to live for the praise of his glory" (Eph. 1:12). What this would mean, then, is that it is in the revelation of God's will for our worship that we discover how he will have us worship him.

This revelation is found all the way through Scripture. We find it, for example, in the precepts of the Law. The Decalogue starts out with four commandments about worship. First, we are to worship and serve but one God; second, our worship is to avoid idolatry; third, it is to glorify God's name; and fourth, it is to remember God's works of creation and redemption on the Sabbath in rest from human works. Then, as an elaboration of this basic law, there is the ceremonial law. While the church has never considered the ceremonial law to be prescriptive for her worship, it has often been studied for its insights into worship. All this liturgical law was expounded by the prophets and exemplified in the worship of Israel. The story of the golden calf and the disobedient sacrifice of Saul make clear what it is not. The prayers of Hannah, David, and Elijah make clear what it is. Above all, we see in Jesus the fulfillment of the rites and ceremonies of the Law. Jesus taught his disciples a great deal about true worship, and he often led them in prayer. He himself was baptized at the hand of John the Baptist. He often broke bread with his disciples, and in the Upper Room he gave them instructions about how they were to continue to break bread as a sacred memorial of his death and resurrection. In the Gospel of John we are taught to worship in Spirit and in truth. The book of Acts gives us several important insights into early Christian worship. We read there of a number of baptisms, and we find a rather thorough description of a daily prayer service. We learn quite a bit from this book about the ministry of the Word and almsgiving. The apostle Paul in his epistles gives us several important passages on prayer, on the sacraments, and on preaching. Chapters 10-14 of his First Epistle to the Corinthians is a virtual treatise on worship. Scattered throughout his various epistles we find

9

all kinds of liturgical material. The Scriptures, both the Old and the New Testaments, are very rich in teaching about worship. It is in God's Word — in the same Word that calls us to worship — that we find the sense of that worship.

We take it as a basic principle of our inquiry, then, that it is to Scripture, first of all, that we must go when we would try to find an answer to our questions about the meaning of worship. That our worship should be according to Scripture is obviously one of the principles that we have inherited from the Protestant Reformation. Early in the Reformation it was expressed by Martin Bucer in his *Grund und Ursach*. It was developed with particular clarity by John Oecolampadius, who distinguished the principle from a naive biblicism. There had been those who felt that worship was biblical as long as nothing was done that was expressly forbidden in Scripture. On the other hand, there were those who insisted that for worship to be biblical, only that could be done which was commanded in Scripture. As Oecolampadius saw it, neither of these approaches is satisfactory. He developed the principle that our worship should be "according to Scripture."[7] To be sure, we do not find a ready-made liturgy in the Bible, but we do find many teachings about worship. In the sacred pages we find all kinds of examples of worship that was genuine, true, and spiritual. We discover general principles for doing things "decently and in order" that we should follow in our worship. That our worship should be according to Scripture is a sound principle.

There is one aspect of the principle that our worship should be according to Scripture that needs particular attention. One of the fascinating things about the New Testament

7. For a detailed study of how Oecolampadius developed the principle of "reformed according to Scripture," see my study *The Shaping of the Reformed Baptismal Rite in the Sixteenth Century* (Grand Rapids: William B. Eerdmans, 1992), pp. 119ff.

teaching on worship is the way it so frequently explains the worship of the New Testament church in terms of the worship of Israel. In the First Epistle of Peter we find that wonderful passage on the worship of the Christian church that speaks of it as a spiritual sacrifice, performed by a royal priesthood, in a spiritual temple not built with human hands (2:4-10). The imagery, quite obviously, is all taken from the Old Testament. It assumes the literary imagery that has been developed through the whole of Scripture. We find another example in the Epistle of James. Elijah is, for the church just as he was for Israel, the example of persistent disciplined prayer (James 5:17-18). For centuries the biblical tradition had developed a list of heroes and heroines of prayer. Prominent on this list were Abraham, Moses, Hannah, Daniel, Esther, and, above all, David. Elijah had a particularly important place on this list. These heroes and heroines were examples of how the devout are to pray. The apostle Paul is constantly explaining the worship of the church by references to the Old Testament. When he wants to speak of baptism, he speaks of the crossing of the Red Sea, and when he wants to speak of the Lord's Supper, he speaks of manna and the water from the rock (1 Cor. 10:1-13). A bit further on he speaks of the cup at the Lord's Supper as the cup of the new covenant, an obvious reference to Exodus 24:8 (1 Cor. 11:25). A generation ago those passages were looked on with embarrassment by many New Testament scholars. It was quite obvious to these scholars that the apostle was using typology, a very outmoded way of explaining Scripture. More recent scholarship exhibits a much deeper appreciation of typology. We realize that typology is a distinct way of understanding things. The New Testament is filled with this approach to understanding, and if we are to understand worship as Jesus and his disciples understood it, we have to work with this typological approach. As the synoptic Gospels present it, Jesus himself set the first celebration of the Supper in the context of the Passover meal (Mark

11

14:12-25 ‖). Even the Gospel of John apparently intends to clothe the celebration of the eucharist with the imagery of Passover (6:4). The Revelation of John is a virtual symphony of typology. All that Revelation says about the transcendent dimension of worship is said in terms of the imagery of the worship of the Temple in Jerusalem. All the way through the New Testament the worship of the church is understood by means of the imagery, the examples, and the types of the Old Testament.

This approach to understanding worship was continued by the church for centuries. The *Didache,* the oldest Christian document we have outside the canonical books of the New Testament, understands Christian worship as the fulfillment of the prophecy of Malachi 1:11 that in the last days God's people will offer pure worship on every shore. The oldest collection of Christian hymns, the *Odes of Solomon,* understands the singing of Christian hymns typologically. That quite obviously is the reason for giving the collection the name it bears. Each hymn in the collection is a pendant of one of the canonical psalms. The same thing is evident in Tertullian's treatise on baptism, written at the end of the second century, which explains the sacrament with reference to a series of Old Testament types of baptism. This is only the first of a whole host of works that explain the sacraments by means of their Old Testament types. The most famous of these was St. Ambrose of Milan's *De sacramentis.* For many centuries after it was introduced, the church used this approach to explain its worship.

Worship has its own imagery and its own language, and that distinct approach to expression is essentially biblical. The vocabulary, the figures, and the rhetoric of worship are all biblical. This was beautifully exemplified almost three hundred years ago by the great biblical commentator Matthew Henry. In his *Method of Prayer,* a work that for generations shaped the prayer life of Protestantism, Henry tried to show

how one could pray in the biblical idiom. This concern for the biblical language of prayer was still strong 150 years ago, when Princeton Seminary's Samuel Miller admonished ministers to adopt the language of Scripture when leading in public prayer.[8] As Miller put it, prayer should "abound in the language of Scripture." In our own day Cardinal Danielou has endorsed the same principle in his famous contribution to the liturgical movement, *Bible et liturgie.*

The value of using the biblical types as a way of understanding the deepest mysteries of the faith has been magnificently illustrated in recent times by the Second Vatican Council's schema on the church, the famous *Lumen gentium,* one of the most effective theological statements of our century. What is remarkable about the *Lumen gentium* is that instead of defining its doctrine of the church in terms of systematic theology, it presents its message in classic biblical imagery. It uses the imagery, the types, the parables, and the figures that the apostles and Jesus himself used to speak of the church: the church is the new Israel, the heavenly Jerusalem, the spiritual Temple, the bride of Christ. It is amazing how effective this kind of theological discussion is!

## III

In seeking to discover what worship is supposed to be, we will certainly do well to reserve a place for the study of liturgical tradition. And yet, as clever as Fr. Kavanagh's *Liturgical Theology* undoubtedly is, he still has not tempted me to trade in *sola scriptura* for *lex orandi lex credendi.* Again I find myself in agreement with Professor Wainwright: liturgical tradition alone can hardly serve as its own norm. There are too many times

8. See Miller, *Thoughts on Public Prayer* (Philadelphia: Presbyterian Board of Publications, 1848), pp. 220ff.

when liturgical practice goes awry. There are too many times when we have to say, Yes, we know what the current practice is, but what we would like to know is what it *should* be. It is at this point, as Wainwright has pointed out, that we turn to Scripture. This does not mean that we should ignore two thousand years of liturgical tradition, however. Like Karl Barth, I am quite happy to acknowledge an authority under the Word.[9] The words and ways of Christian tradition often expound Scripture magnificently.

Protestant worship has borrowed heavily from patristic tradition, a point I have made elsewhere in considerable detail.[10] Here, let it suffice to point to the tremendous influence of such patristic preachers as Origen, John Chrysostom, and Augustine on the liturgical preaching of the Reformation. The popular psalmody and hymnody of the ancient church were an inspiration to the Reformers, as were patristic prayer disciplines. The restoration of catechetical instruction was another obvious example of the patristic roots of Protestant worship.

The Protestant Reformers were quite happy to speak of the Fathers of the ancient church as *testes veritatis,* "witnesses to the truth." They spoke of the Fathers in their day much as we speak of the Reformers in our day. For us the Fathers and the Reformers have places of special honor in the tradition, but there are others who need to be included. If we are to explain Protestant worship as it is practiced in America today, we need to do more than study the Reformation. Much of the best in Protestant worship came not from the Reformers but from the Puritans, who gave special attention to deepening the life of prayer and developing the discipline of daily worship

9. Barth, *Church Dogmatics,* 4 vols., ed. Thomas F. Torrance, trans. Geoffrey W. Bromiley (Edinburgh: T. & T. Clark, 1936-69), I/2: 585-660.
10. See my book *Patristic Roots of Reformed Worship* (Zurich: TVZ, 1975).

in the family. Even as early as the seventeenth century, the first generation of American ministers set to work shaping and reshaping the worship of American Protestantism. The first book printed in America, the Bay Psalter, was a liturgical book. With the coming of the Great Awakening, Pietism began to have its effect. John Wesley translated the hymns of the German Pietists, and his brother Charles penned a tremendous collection of hymns, one of the classics of Christian doxology. Herrenhut, the Pietist utopia of Count Zinzendorf, has had almost as much influence on the worship of the American church as either Wittenberg or Geneva. In the nineteenth century, Romanticism began to take worship in other directions — frontier revivals on the one hand and the "High Church" movement on the other. They were both the products of Romanticism, although working in very different directions. Then came Charles Haddon Spurgeon, Claus Harms, Alphonse Monod, and Alexander Whyte, who provided the world with most extraordinary examples of preaching. Their virtuosity was so great that it eclipsed all the rest of worship, even though they led in prayer with exemplary devotion and often championed the weekly celebration of the Lord's Supper. We are still too close to these giants to evaluate them, and yet we can hardly leave them out of our consideration. The cloud of witnesses we must gather about us is indeed vast.

There is one way in which the searching out of the Protestant liturgical heritage differs from the studies of other traditions. Here we will interest ourselves less in sacramentaries and lectionaries than in hymnbooks and sermons. It has often been said that the hymnbook is the Protestant missal. There is quite a bit of truth to this. As James White has recently pointed out, Protestant liturgical books are of a distinct character.[11] Rather than following an actual liturgical text, the

11. See White, *Protestant Worship: Traditions in Transition* (Louisville: Westminster/John Knox Press, 1989), pp. 13-15.

15

typical American Protestant minister for the last three centuries has been expected to "conceive" prayers appropriate to the time and place. There have been books to help the minister in this most prophetic of ministries, and there are some records of actual prayers, such as those in Richard Baxter's *Reformed Liturgy* and Matthew Henry's *Method of Prayer.* A study of these documents will do much to help us understand the worship of the period. Public prayer was highly valued in Puritan worship. Those who had the gift of leading in prayer were particularly respected, and there were obviously many who were able to develop this gift. But again we are very much aware that Luther's sermons on prayer tell us more than the prayers he is known to have composed. The documents we have will require very careful reading in order to get at the experience behind the document, but then liturgical scholars of all sorts have similar problems. The formal documents are at best only part of the evidence.

Having made these introductory remarks, I would now like to look at five biblical types of doxology. Following the title, I will present them as five musical themes sounded clearly in the Old Testament and then fully developed in the New Testament. Then we will consider the long tradition of Christian worship to note a series of variations which age after age, people after people, have developed on these themes. It is in this way that we will consider the themes and variations of a Christian doxology.

16

# II

## Epicletic Doxology

Epiclesis is one of the basic acts of worship. Epiclesis is calling on the name of the Lord; it is invocation. In fact, one might better use the word *invocation* than *epiclesis* if it were not that *epiclesis* is an established term in the discussion of worship. Basically the word *epiclesis* means "to call upon, to make an appeal to someone or address oneself to someone." When the faithful call upon God in time of need, God is glorified. The very act of calling upon God's name is itself worship. Just as it is one of the basic commandments of the Law not to take God's name in vain, so it is basic in the gospel that we are to hallow God's name.

When the third commandment teaches us, "You shall not take the name of the LORD your God in vain" (Exod. 20:7), it recognizes that calling on God's name, or invoking God's name in the making of vows or in the offering of prayer, is an act of worship. In the biblical idiom, prophesying in God's name, praising God's name, and blessing and sanctifying God's name all have to do with worship.[1] What the commandment forbids

---

1. On the significance of the third commandment, see Brevard S. Childs, *The Book of Exodus* (Philadelphia: Westminster Press, 1974), pp. 409-12; and Johs. Pedersen, *Israel: Its Life and Culture*, 4 vols. (London: Oxford University Press, 1959), I-II: 245-59.

17

is a vain, insincere, or empty worship. When Jesus taught the disciples the Lord's Prayer, he put the third commandment positively: "Hallowed be thy name" (Matt. 6:9). This means that we are to honor God's name in our worship. We are not to use God's name carelessly, but rather we are to use it as a means of calling upon God in prayer; we are to use it in supplication, adoration, and awe. When the faithful utter God's name, it should be a confession of faith that bears witness to our faith in God and therefore honors him.

A classic example of epiclesis is the prayer of the children of Israel in Egypt. It was a very particular kind of prayer. Appearing to Moses in the burning bush, God said, "And now, behold, the cry of the people of Israel has come to me" (Exod. 3:9). The prayer is a cry. Because of their bondage, the worship of the children of Israel became a complaint or lamentation. This we must understand as a positive development. It is not when things are going well that the value of communion with God appears. It is when we discover our real nature, our frailty — when we discover that we are creatures of need — that we finally discover who God really is. In their slavery the Israelites had turned to the half-remembered traditions of the God of Abraham, Isaac, and Jacob and appealed to that God for their salvation, and in this God was glorified. No longer was worship a polite respect due to their Creator. Because of their suffering, it became an impassioned cry to their Redeemer.

The psalms of lamentation are epiclesis. One often hears surprise that the Psalms, the canonical collection of Hebrew doxology, has such a large number of lamentations.[2] This,

2. The pioneering work of Hermann Gunkel has produced a profusion of studies that have given us considerable insight into the prayers of lamentation found in Scripture. Among the most helpful are the following: J. Bergreich, "Das priesterliche Heilsorakel," *Zeitschrift zum alttestamentlichen Wissenschaft* 52 (1934): 81-92; Walter Beyerlin, "Die tôda der Heilsvergegenwärtigung in den Klageliedern des Einzelen," *Zeitschrift zum alttestamentlichen Wissenschaft* 79 (1968): 208-24; John Bright, "A Prophet's

however, only reflects the fact that much of the worship of the Temple in Jerusalem, even from earliest times, was devoted to laying out before God the needs of Israel. Solomon's prayer of dedication makes this very clear (1 Kings 8:23-61). The Temple is dedicated as a house of prayer to which Israel is to come in time of drought, in time of famine, in time of military defeat, and in time of personal disaster. Days of fasting were observed in the Temple as much as days of feasting. A good number of the psalms were intended for use at these fast-day observances. The Temple was not only for public worship, to be sure. As Hannah went to Shiloh and wept bitterly before the Lord, thousands of people must have come to the Temple in Jerusalem to pour out their personal sorrows (1 Sam. 1:1-28). There were psalms intended for this purpose as well. In fact, many of the most beautiful psalms were intended to bring to God the personal sorrows of individual worshipers. Psalm 6 is the lamentation of one suffering from serious illness who wonders if the end of life is upon him.

> O LORD, rebuke me not in thy anger,
>   nor chasten me in thy wrath.
> Be gracious to me, O LORD, for I am languishing;
>   O LORD, heal me, for my bones are troubled.
> My soul also is sorely troubled.
>   But thou, O LORD — how long?

---

Lament and Its Answer: Jeremiah 15:10-21," *Interpretation* 28 (1974): 75-88; Hans-Joachim Kraus, *Worship in Israel: A Cultic History of the Old Testament,* trans. G. Buswell (Oxford: Basil Blackwell, 1966), pp. 218-22; Sigmund Mowinckel, *The Psalms in Israel's Worship,* 2 vols. (Nashville: Abingdon Press, 1962), 1: 195-219 and 2: 9-11; Hans Schmidt, *Die Psalmen,* Handbuch zum alten Testament 15 (Tübingen: J. C. B. Mohr, 1934); Arthur Weiser, *The Psalms* (Philadelphia: Westminster Press, 1962), pp. 66-83; and Claus Westermann, *Praise and Lament in the Psalms,* trans. Keith R. Crim and Richard N. Soulen (Atlanta: John Knox Press, 1981), pp. 165-213.

Turn, O LORD, save my life;
  deliver me for the sake of thy steadfast love.
For in death there is no remembrance of thee;
  in Sheol who can give thee praise?

I am weary with my moaning;
  every night I flood my bed with tears;
  I drench my couch with my weeping. (Vv. 1-6)

Worship, as we see from such psalms, is not limited to celebration, nor is it spoiled by tears, as some of our more upbeat contemporaries would tell us.

When we look at the psalms of lamentation, we notice that they make a point of calling upon the name of the Lord.[3] An invocation names the God to whom we pray. It is not simply an appeal to whatever transcendent powers there might be. In earlier times the tetragram would have been consciously pronounced. "In thee, O LORD, do I seek refuge" (Ps. 31:1). "Out of the depths I cry to thee, O LORD!" (130:1). These psalms typically insist that it is the Lord, not some other god, to whom the worshiper turns in need. One notices this again and again as one prays through the Psalter. "Give ear to my words, O LORD; give heed to my groaning. Hearken to the sound of my cry, my King and my God, for to thee do I pray" (5:1-2). The invocation of God by the tetragram is a confession of Israel's monotheistic faith. It is of the very essence of invocation to call on the name of the Lord.

Psalm 102 is a particularly fine example of the lamentation. The first two verses are an invocation calling upon the name of the LORD:

Hear my prayer, O LORD;
  let my cry come to thee!

3. Mowinckel is still helpful on the relation of invocation and lamentation; see *The Psalms in Israel's Worship,* 1: 195ff.

Do not hide thy face from me
 in the day of my distress!
Incline thy ear to me;
 answer me speedily in the day when I call!

Then the next nine verses lay out a full description of one's sorrow in the form of a meditation. It looks at that sorrow very honestly, open to all the pain. Rather than covering over the devastation, the lamentation searches it all out and confesses it.

For my days pass away like smoke,
 and my bones burn like a furnace.
My heart is smitten like grass, and withered;
 I forget to eat my bread.
Because of my loud groaning
 my bones cleave to my flesh.
I am like a vulture of the wilderness,
 like an owl of the waste places;
I lie awake,
 I am like a lonely bird on the housetop.
All the day my enemies taunt me,
 those who deride me use my name for a curse.
For I eat ashes like bread,
 and mingle tears with my drink,
because of thy indignation and anger;
 for thou hast taken me up and thrown me away.
My days are like an evening shadow;
 I wither away like grass. (Vv. 3-11)

When the godly weep, they weep unto God, and weeping before God is worship just as much as rejoicing before God.

In Psalms 42–43 we have the same detailed lamentation. The imagery of lamentation makes vivid the worshiper's plaint. The hart, or perhaps more graphically the antelope or impala of the arid regions of Africa and Asia, hunting for the few streams or water holes which that dry land offers is an effective figure for the troubled soul. The same is true of the imagery of the insistent, unrelenting waves of despair and the dark depths of depression. Then the poetic device of the refrain heightens even more this expression of devout sorrow, as the complaint is repeated over and over again as a chorus.

> As a hart longs
>   for flowing streams,
> so longs my soul
>   for thee, O God.
> My soul thirsts for God,
>   for the living God.
> When shall I come and behold
>   the face of God?
> My tears have been my food
>   day and night,
> while men say to me continually,
>   "Where is your God?" . . .
>
>     Why are you cast down, O my soul,
>       and why are you disquieted within me?
>     Hope in God; for I shall again praise him,
>       my help and my God.
>
> My soul is cast down within me,
>   therefore I remember thee
> from the land of Jordan and of Hermon,
>   from Mount Mizar.
> Deep calls to deep
>   at the thunder of thy cataracts;
> all thy waves and thy billows
>   have gone over me. . . .
>
> I say to God, my rock:
>   "Why hast thou forgotten me?
> Why go I mourning

because of the oppression of the enemy?"
As with a deadly wound in my body,
    my adversaries taunt me,
while they say to me continually,
    "Where is your God?"

        Why are you cast down, O my soul,
            and why are you disquieted within me?
        Hope in God; for I shall again praise him,
            my help and my God. (Ps. 42)

This psalm and the psalm that follows it must originally have
been the same prayer, because the same chorus is repeated. If
this is indeed the case, then the detailed lamentation of the
first psalm is followed by a prayer for deliverance. In the
second it is a prayer filled with hope, as the chorus emphasizes.

Vindicate me, O God, and defend my cause
    against an ungodly people;
from deceitful and unjust men
    deliver me!
For thou art the God in whom I take refuge;
    why hast thou cast me off?
Why go I mourning
    because of the oppression of the enemy?

Oh send out thy light and thy truth;
    let them lead me,
let them bring me to thy holy hill
    and to thy dwelling!
Then I will go to the altar of God,
    to God my exceeding joy;
and I will praise thee with the lyre,
    O God, my God.

        Why are you cast down, O my soul,
            and why are you disquieted within me?

23

> Hope in God; for I shall again praise him,
>> my help and my God. (Ps. 43)

When God's people fix their hope in God, then God is honored.

Very often these psalms of lamentation move from the pouring out of one's troubles to a profound confession of faith. This movement is one of their most important characteristics. Psalms of lamentation often become psalms of confidence. We notice this particularly in Psalm 22:

> My God, my God, why hast thou forsaken me?
>> Why art thou so far from helping me, from the words
>>> of my groaning?
> O my God, I cry by day, but thou dost not answer;
>> and by night, but find no rest.

> Yet thou art holy,
>> enthroned on the praises of Israel.
> In thee our fathers trusted;
>> they trusted, and thou didst deliver them.
> To thee they cried, and were saved;
>> in thee they trusted, and were not disappointed.
>>>> (Vv. 1-5)

In the praying of this psalm, one moves from despair to faith as one meditates on one's troubles in the light of God's saving glory. It is of the very nature of the God who reveals himself in Scripture that he calls us to bring him our sorrows. The God of the Bible is not inclined to dwell in some unperturbed Olympian calm. Jesus made this particularly clear when he taught, "Come to me, all who labor and are heavy laden, and I will give you rest" (Matt. 11:28). The god of the philosophers may not want to hear of the troubles of the world, but it is not the god of the philosophers whom we worship. It is for this reason, of course, that Jesus made such a point of teaching his

24

disciples to invoke God with the new tetragram, ABBA, in place of the old tetragram, YHWH (6:9). Just as human fathers find satisfaction in being able to supply the needs of their children, so our heavenly Father is worshiped when we bring our needs to him.

For Jesus the epicletic nature of worship was particularly important. The Lord's Prayer makes clear that the bringing of our needs to God is central to Christian worship. As I once heard Ernst Käsemann insist, the Lord's Prayer is a beggar's prayer. It yearns for the coming of the kingdom, seeks daily bread, implores the forgiveness of sin, begs release from temptation and deliverance from evil. One notices this above all in Christ's supreme act of worship on the cross. During his Passion, Jesus constantly prayed the lamentations of Israel as he fulfilled the role of the suffering servant. In his prayer on the cross, Jesus offered up the classic laments of Israel. He prayed the psalms of lamentation that Israel had prayed for untold generations. That was an essential dimension of his priestly ministry. He prayed Psalm 22 ("My God, my God, why hast thou forsaken me?"), Psalm 42 ("My soul thirsts for God, for the living God"), and Psalm 31 ("Into thy hand I commit my spirit"). These psalms, which yearn for God's presence, are of the very essence of epiclesis. God's glory is tacitly confessed by our thirst, our unquenchable desire for God, which none other can satisfy.

The prayer that is in the name of Jesus is a supplication for the coming of the kingdom. As we find it in the Upper Room discourse of the Gospel of John, it is a supplication for the unity, vitality, purity, and continuity of the church (John 14–17). It has been poured out under the threefold promise that when it is offered up in the name of Jesus, it is heard by the Father in heaven (14:13; 15:16; 16:23-24). What Jesus teaches us here is that by such prayer the Father is glorified. The early disciples understood themselves to have a ministry of intercessory prayer (Acts 6:4; 1 Tim. 2:1-8). They believed that Jesus himself had given them this ministry. Praying in the name of Jesus was in a very real sense continuing the ministry that Jesus had begun. It was of the very essence of the spiritual priesthood that Christians knew themselves to have been called to offer (1 Pet. 2:4-9).

That prayer in time of need is indeed worship has constantly been illustrated through the history of Christian worship. One of the most detailed pictures of the service of worship as it was celebrated in the ancient church is found in the eighth book of the *Apostolic Constitutions.* This document reflects the liturgical life of Antioch toward the last half of the fourth century. From it we get the impression that a good portion of time was given to presenting the needs of the congregation to God. As cate-chumens, energumens, and penitents were in turn dismissed, elaborate prayers were said for them that they might be en-lightened by the truth, that they might be freed from the powers of darkness, and that they might enter the full communion of the church. Individuals presented themselves to the bishop for the laying on of hands, and with that the whole congregation prayed, "Lord have mercy on this thy servant!" Once all these people had been prayed for, blessed, and dismissed, the faithful began the classic intercessions for the church, for her ministers, for all peoples, for kings and those in authority, for the peace of the world and the relief of the suffering. There are prayers for those who are traveling, those involved in trade, for virgins, widows, and women bearing children. Hardly anything is left unmen-tioned, and one can well imagine that at least half an hour was given to these prayers. The faithful who devoted themselves to such elaborate supplications obviously believed that God is worshiped when his people bring their needs to him. The worship described in the *Apostolic Constitutions,* although it may be described in greater detail than most of the documents we have from this period, no doubt gives us a picture of what typically happened in the public prayers of the ancient church. A consid-erable amount of time was given to supplication.

26

This dimension of Christian worship is particularly clear in the Benedictine daily office, so essential to the doxology of the medieval church. Many of the offices begin with the classic invocation, "Be pleased, O God, to deliver me! O LORD, make haste to help me!" (Ps. 70:1). The very fact that according to the rule of St. Benedict the whole Psalter was prayed through in the course of a week meant that all these psalms of lamentation were regularly prayed through in worship.[4] Even before St. Benedict, Psalm 63 had become the central prayer of the morning office.[5] The themes of invocation are beautifully unfolded:

> O God, thou art my God, early in the morning I seek thee,
> my soul thirsts for thee;
> my flesh faints for thee,
> as in a dry and weary land where no water is.
> So have I looked upon thee in the sanctuary,
> beholding thy power and glory.
> Because thy steadfast love is better than life,
> my lips will praise thee.
> So I will bless thee as long as I live;
> I will lift up my hands and call on thy name.
>
> (Ps. 63:1-4)[6]

In the monasteries influenced by the Cluniac reform, the Benedictine office was elaborated with a generous use of the

---

4. See *The Rule of St. Benedict,* Latin text with English translation by Justin McCann (Westminster, Md.: Newman Press, 1952), pp. 49-69. On the details of the daily office, see *La règle de saint Benoît, texte et commentaire historique et critique,* by Adalbert de Vogüé (Paris: Les Éditions du Cerf, 1971), pp. 483ff. and 545ff.

5. We find this already in the *Apostolic Constitutions,* 8.37. For a study of the earliest traditions of morning prayer, see Juan Mateos, *De officio matutino et vespero in ritibus orientalibus* (Rome: Athenaeum Sancti Anselmi, 1969).

6. Historically, the phrase "early in the morning," which is found in the Septuagint and the Vulgate but not in the Hebrew, has commended this psalm for morning prayer.

penitential psalms, which intensified the epicletic aspect of medieval doxology.[7] Finally, according to the rule of St. Benedict, each office came to its climax with the *Kyrie eleison,* "Lord have mercy, Christ have mercy, Lord have mercy." This prayer, too, is an invocation, even if it comes toward the end of the service. Wherever the Benedictine office has been maintained, the epicletic foundation of worship has remained solid.

It was at the Council of Florence that the epiclesis became a matter of controversy between the Eastern church and the Western church. In the celebration of the eucharist, the Orthodox had always given great importance to the invocation of the Holy Spirit that the bread and wine become the body and blood of Christ and that the congregation be sanctified by the divine presence. This, as the Orthodox understood it, prevented the liturgy from becoming a magical ceremony in which by the repetition of the words of consecration the bread and wine were turned into the body and blood of Christ. A great number of things were at play that need not concern us here, but this discussion was of a highly symbolic nature. It has to do with the humility of our worship. What the Orthodox were really insisting upon was the frailty of the human condition. In Florence, at the height of the Renaissance, the Orthodox prophetically insisted that God's redemptive power is not at our disposal but is entirely dependent on the work of God's Spirit within us.

The Reformation brought a reform of prayer life that was just as important as its reform of doctrine. The medieval monastery had devoted itself to prayer, and its various orders developed innumerable disciplines of prayer that stand today as a witness to the "Age of Faith." By the beginning of the sixteenth century, much of this venerable tradition had broken down.

In contrast to the elaborate disciplines of prayer developed by the mystics of the Middle Ages, the approach that developed

7. See Bede K. Lackner, *The Eleventh-Century Background of Cîteaux* (Washington: Consortium Press, 1972), pp. 42-52.

out of the Reformation was very simple. The monasteries and religious communities tended to regard mental prayer as superior to prayer concerning practical needs and worries. It was only natural that Luther as well as the other Reformers began to rethink prayer in terms of the great numbers of ordinary people who lived in the world and fully entered into the cares and worries of family life and the concerns of community welfare. More and more Luther began to see prayer as an act of faith. Prayer believes the promises of God. The Scriptures are filled with divine promises of God's care for his people in time of need. Again and again, Luther reminds us, Jesus himself promised that if we would present our needs to the Father in our prayers, they would be heard. To do this, Luther taught, was to live by faith.[8] In poverty and fallibility, the state in which all of us actually live, we trust in God. We are creatures of need, and our need is for God. In our lamentations, our supplications, and our calling on God's name in time of need, we recognize this, and in this recognition God is glorified.

Another place the Reformation showed a deep perception of the epicletic dimension of worship was in the celebration of baptism. In the *German Baptismal Book* of 1523, Luther emphasized the importance of the prayers of those who attend the baptism of a child. It was important, as Luther saw it, that the baptismal service be celebrated in the language of the people so that they could participate in the prayers of the service. For the new German baptismal service Luther composed a very fine baptismal invocation, the famous Great Flood Prayer. This prayer asks that just as God had saved Noah and his family at the time of the Great Flood and had saved the children of Israel from Egypt by bringing them through the Red Sea, he might save the child being baptized.

---

8. Luther, "On Rogationtide Prayer," in *Luther's Works*, 55 vols., ed. Jaroslav Pelikan and Helmut T. Lehmann (Philadelphia: Fortress Press, 1955-), 42: 85-93.

Almighty eternal God, who according to Thy righteous judgment didst condemn the unbelieving world through the flood and in Thy great mercy didst preserve believing Noah and his family, and who didst drown hardhearted Pharaoh with all his host in the Red Sea and didst lead Thy people Israel through the same on dry ground, thereby prefiguring this bath of Thy baptism, and who through the baptism of Thy dear Child, our Lord Jesus Christ, hast consecrated and set apart the Jordan and all water as a salutary flood and a rich and full washing away of sins: We pray through Thy same groundless mercy that Thou wilt graciously behold this N. and bless him with true faith in the spirit so that by means of this saving flood all that has been born in him from Adam and which he himself has added thereto may be drowned in him and engulfed, and that he may be sundered from the number of the unbelieving, preserved dry and secure in the holy ark of Christendom, serve Thy name at all times fervent in spirit and joyful in hope, so that with all believers he may be made worthy to attain eternal life according to Thy promise; through Jesus Christ our Lord. Amen.[9]

Shortly after this, Martin Bucer, the Reformer of Strasbourg, wrote a baptismal invocation that deepened the concept even more. Bucer's baptismal invocation asks that by the work of the Holy Spirit the spiritual cleansing and new birth signified by the outward washing with water might be accomplished inwardly in the hearts of those being baptized.

Almighty eternal God, merciful Father, seeing that the righteous shall live by faith alone and seeing that it is impossible to be pleasing to you except by faith, so we pray you would grant the gift of faith to this child, who is of your creation. Seal and

9. English translation from *Luther's Works,* 53: 97. For a further study of this prayer, see my book *The Shaping of the Reformed Baptismal Rite in the Sixteenth Century* (Grand Rapids: William B. Eerdmans, 1992), pp. 227-34.

confirm him by the presence of the Holy Spirit in his heart, according to the promise of your Son, in order that there might be that inward renewal and rebirth of the spirit through this our outward baptism of water, seeing that this is indeed its true meaning; and that as he is baptized into the death of Christ Jesus, buried with him, and through him awakened from the dead so grant that he walk in a new life, to the praise of God's glory and to the profit of his neighbor. Amen.[10]

Essentially what Bucer did was to apply the insights of the Greek Orthodox theologians at the Council of Florence to the celebration of the sacrament of baptism. But also there is another thing at play here. Lamentation, the confession of sin, and the appeal to God for a new heart and spirit are very strong elements in baptism. In baptism we cry out to God for a new and holy life. In baptism above all it is made clear that crying to God in time of need is indeed the worship God would have from us.

John Calvin understood invocation to be one of the essential duties Christians owe to God. In fact, he gives us a good definition: " 'Invocation' is that habit of our mind, whenever necessity presses us, of resorting to [God's] faithfulness and help as our only support."[11] Calvin goes on to affirm that prayer is the chief exercise of our faith because in prayer we bring our needs to God, who is the only one sufficient to supply our need. Supplications to God about our daily needs are not some sort of lower level of prayer. To call on God for help is to confess our faith both in his power to come to our aid and in his willingness to save us from our distress.[12] The

10. For a study of this text, see my book *The Shaping of the Reformed Baptismal Rite in the Sixteenth Century,* p. 234.

11. Calvin, *Institutes of the Christian Religion,* Library of Christian Classics, vols. 20-21, trans. Ford Lewis Battles, ed. John T. McNeill (Philadelphia: Westminster Press, 1960), 2.8.16.

12. See Calvin, *Institutes,* 3.20.11.

ordinary service of worship in Geneva began with the invocation "Our help is in the name of the Lord who made heaven and earth." This was followed by a confession of sin and supplication for mercy that for the sake of Christ and through the inner working of the Holy Spirit we might bear the fruits of the new life.[13] The confession of sin belonged to epiclesis for Calvin, because it is in the midst of our sin that God's Spirit brings us to prayer. In spite of our sin and even in contradiction to our sin, "God has sent the Spirit of his Son into our hearts, crying, 'Abba! Father!'" (Gal. 4:6). For Calvin epiclesis was the crying out of God's Spirit in our hearts that proves us to be God's children.

The piety of classical Protestantism taught the importance of bringing our needs to God in prayer. This was underlined in the catechisms used to teach the common people. The major Protestant catechisms all gave considerable attention to the interpretation of the Lord's Prayer. Luther's Catechism, the catechism found in the Anglican Book of Common Prayer, the Heidelberg Catechism, and the Westminster Shorter Catechism all teach the value of bringing our sorrows and needs before God in prayer. The Anglican Catechism puts it very briefly but nevertheless makes the Protestant emphasis quite clear.

*Catechist.* My good Child, know this; that thou art not able to do these things of thyself, nor to walk in the Commandments of God, and to serve him, without his special grace; which thou must learn at all times to call for by diligent prayer. Let me hear, therefore, if thou canst say the Lord's Prayer.

*Answer.* Our Father, who art in heaven, Hallowed be thy Name. Thy kingdom come. Thy will be done, on

13. See John Calvin, *La forme des prieres et chantz ecclesiastiques,* in *Joannis Calvini opera selecta,* vol. 2, ed. Dora Scheuner (Munich: Chr. Kaiser, 1952), pp. 18ff.

earth as it is in heaven. Give us this day our daily bread. And forgive us our trespasses, As we forgive those who trespass against us. And lead us not into temptation, but deliver us from evil. Amen.

*Catechist.* What desirest thou of God in this Prayer?

*Answer.* I desire my Lord God, our heavenly Father, who is the giver of all goodness, to send his grace unto me, and to all people; that we may worship him, serve him, and obey him, as we ought to do. And I pray unto God, that he will send us all things that are needful both for our souls and bodies; and that he will be merciful unto us, and forgive us our sins; and that it will please him to save and defend us in all dangers both of soul and body; and that he will keep us from all sin and wickedness, and from our spiritual enemy, and from everlasting death. And this I trust he will do of his mercy and goodness, through our Lord Jesus Christ. And therefore I say, Amen, so be it. *(The Book of Common Prayer)*

This catechism was directed toward the needs of the ploughmen, kitchen maids, and shopkeepers of England. It teaches them to lay their most common needs as well as their deepest religious yearnings before God. It was not mental prayer that was taught but practical prayer.

Psalms and prayers of lamentation came to occupy a significant place in Protestant psalters and hymnbooks. One thinks particularly of Clement Marot's setting of Psalm 6 in the *Genevan Psalter* of 1542. Marot, who was the most sparkling French lyric poet of the sixteenth century, had put the psalm into French meter during a serious illness. It was therefore very personal poetry, and yet it soon became liturgical

33

poetry. Marot's metrical versions of the psalms are an amazing combination of careful translation of the biblical text and lyrical poetic form. Marot's genius eludes translators, but the following may be helpful nevertheless.

> O LORD, do not thou chide me,
> Nor in thy wrath chastise me,
> To me be gracious, LORD!
> See thou how much I languish;
> O heal me from my anguish;
> My bones are troubled sore.

> My soul is troubled greatly.
> O hasten thou to aid me.
> Why dost thou tarry, LORD?
> Be thou my strong Preserver,
> For thy love's sake deliver,
> According to thy Word!

> How may the dead adore thee
> Or bring their thanks before thee
> Or praise thy holy Name?
> I'm weary with my moaning,
> And spend my time in groaning;
> I'm overcome with shame.

> Each night, instead of sleeping,
> I drench my couch with weeping;
> For grief my eyes grow weak,
> Since foes with hate surround me
> And without ceasing hound me;
> My ruin they all seek.

> Depart from me, transgressors.
> Flee now, all you oppressors:
> The LORD did heed my cry!

He heard my imploration,
Answered my supplication
And with his help is nigh.

The LORD heard when I pleaded
And my appeals he heeded.
My foes shall be ashamed;
They shall be sorely frighted;
Their rout thou hast incited;
Their doom thou hast proclaimed.[14]

Among the French Huguenots of the seventeenth century, this metrical psalm was beloved not only in family prayer but in public worship as well.[15] In the Netherlands the metrical version of Psalm 137, "By the Waters of Babylon," was another supplication used frequently in both public worship and private devotion. Here again the typology is an important element, as those who sang this psalm prayed about their problems in remembering the sorrows of Israel in the Babylonian captivity and God's having delivered them from that captivity.

Highly respected among the hymnodists of Protestant orthodoxy was Paul Gerhardt (1607-1676), pastor of St. Nicholas Church in Berlin. Probably no hymn writer has left so many hymns to the current usage of German churches. Gerhardt's hymns cover the full range of hymnic types from psalm

14. *Book of Praise, Anglo-Genevan Psalter* (Burlington, Ont.: Committee for the Publication of the Anglo-Genevan Psalter, 1972), pp. 9-10. This is not, strictly speaking, a translation of Marot's psalm, but it does use his metrical structure.

15. See the beautiful article of Elizabeth Achtemeier, "Overcoming the World: An Exposition of Psalm 6," *Interpretation* 28 (1974): 75-88. For an appreciation of Marot's work on the *Genevan·Psalter,* see Lenselink, *Les psaumes de Clément Marot. Édition critique du plus ancien text . . . précédée d'une étude par Samuel Jan Lenselink* (Assen: Van Gorcum, 1969).

paraphrases to hymns for the principal Christian feasts. Among his hymns of supplication, one in particular gives us a rich insight into the epicletic nature of worship:

Holy Ghost, dispel our sadness,
    Pierce the clouds of sinful night;
Come, thou source of sweetest gladness,
    Breathe thy life, and spread thy light.
Loving Spirit, God of peace,
    Great distributor of grace,
Rest upon this congregation;
    Hear, O hear our supplication.

From that height which knows no measure,
    As a gracious show'r descend;
Bringing down the richest treasure
    Man can wish, or God can send.
O thou Glory, shining down
    From the Father and the Son,
Grant us thine illumination;
    Rest upon this congregation.

Come, thou best of all donations
    God can give, or we implore;
Having thy sweet consolations
    We need wish for nothing more.
Come with unction and with pow'r,
    On our souls thy graces show'r;
Author of the new creation,
    Make our hearts thy habitation.[16]

16. This translation is credited to John Christian Jacobi and Augustus Toplady. Toplady, a distinguished eighteenth-century theologian, is well known for his classic hymn "Rock of Ages." An amended version is found in several more recent hymnals, including *The Worshipbook* (Philadelphia: Westminster Press, 1975), #419. Gerhardt's original, "Heiliger Geist, du Tröster mein," is found in numerous contemporary German hymnals.

This hymn is a prayer that our worship not be guilty of using God's name in vain, that it not be merely outward worship but inward, Spirit-filled worship. One often accuses Protestant orthodoxy of being aridly scholastic. Nothing could be less true, as is so very clear from this hymn. One notices here a highly developed doctrine of the Holy Spirit, something that is at the core of the epicletic dimension of Christian worship. The invocations and supplications of Christian prayer all finally resolve, as we see in Gerhardt's hymn, to the simple prayer, "Come, Holy Spirit."

It was in the seventeenth century, the century after the Reformation, that Protestant theology began to produce many of its most mature devotional insights. This was particularly true among the Puritans, who were much concerned with the development of the disciplines of prayer. The Puritans had a keen sense of the epicletic nature of prayer. As we find in the *Westminster Directory for Worship,* the Puritans liked to begin the service of worship with a highly developed prayer of invocation that hallowed God's name, gloried in the divine majesty, and bowed down in humility and confession before the throne of grace. This invocation constituted the worshiping assembly in the name of Christ, recalling that wherever two or three be gathered together in his name he is present. For the Puritans, epiclesis had an important place at the celebration of the Lord's Supper. They were, of course, familiar with the discussion of the problem of the eucharistic epiclesis at the Council of Florence in the fifteenth century. Richard Baxter's *Reformed Liturgy* of 1661, which gives us about as good an idea of how the Puritans prayed as any document we possess, includes a eucharistic epiclesis that entreats the Holy Spirit to sanctify the congregation, unite it in love, strengthen it in praise, confirm it in obedience, and seal it unto eternal life.

Most Holy Spirit, proceeding from the Father and the Son: by whom Christ was conceived; by whom the prophets and apos-

37

tles were inspired, and the ministers of Christ are qualified and called: that dwellest and workest in all the members of Christ, whom thou sanctifiest to the image and for the service of their Head, and comfortest them that they may shew forth his praise: illuminate us, that by faith we may see him that is here represented to us. Soften our hearts, and humble us for our sins. Sanctify and quicken us, that we may relish the spiritual food, and feed on it to our nourishment and growth in grace. Shed abroad the love of God upon our hearts, and draw them out in love to him. Fill us with thankfulness and holy joy, and with love to one another. Comfort us by witnessing that we are the children of God. Confirm us for new obedience. Be the earnest of our inheritance, and seal us up to everlasting life. Amen.[17]

For the Puritans, a eucharistic epiclesis was a prayer that through the work of the Holy Spirit the grace signified by the sacrament might be realized in the life of the faithful. Epiclesis entails sanctification, and that made it of surpassing importance for the Puritans. It seeks the presence of God. It is a hungering and thirsting for righteousness that by the benediction of Christ is beatitude.

In the work of the Wesleys, the labors of Richard Baxter bore abundant fruit. In fact, both Baxter and Martin Bucer have often been interpreted as precursors of the Methodist movement. Charles Wesley's hymn to be sung before the reading of the Scriptures might well be called an epiclesis of the reading and preaching of the Scriptures:

Come, Holy Ghost, our hearts inspire,
    Let us thine influence prove,
Source of the old prophetic fire,
    Fountain of life and love.

17. Baxter, *The Reformed Liturgy,* in *The Practical Works of the Rev. Richard Baxter,* 23 vols., ed. William Orme (London: James Duncan, 1830), 15: 480-81.

Come, Holy Ghost (for moved by thee
  The prophets wrote and spoke);
Unlock the truth, thyself the key,
  Unseal the sacred book.

Expand thy wings, celestial dove,
  Brood o'er our nature's night;
On our disordered spirits move,
  And let there now be light.

God through himself we then shall know,
  If thou within us shine;
And sound, with all thy saints below,
  The depths of love divine.[18]

In this profound prayer for illumination, we find the cry for truth transformed into the praise of God.

In its simplest and most profound form, the doxology of fallible humanity is expressed in the spirituals of American blacks. As I have already suggested, nothing exemplifies the prayer of lamentation quite as well as the cry of the children of Israel in Egypt. The blacks took up this cry in its typological setting and turned it into a profound expression of human lamentation:

Go down, Moses,
  'Way down in Egypt land,
Tell ole Pharaoh,
  To let my people go.

---

18. Charles Wesley, *Hymns and Sacred Poems* (London: Strahan, 1740), pp. 42ff. I am indebted to my colleague S. T. Kimbrough for guidance in finding the original sources of Wesley's hymns. For a good, accessible edition of the hymns of the Wesleys, see *John and Charles Wesley: Selected Writings and Hymns,* Classics of Western Spirituality, ed. Frank Whaling (New York: Paulist Press, 1981).

When Israel was in Egypt land:
    Let my people go,
Oppressed so hard they could not stand,
    Let my people go.

"Thus spoke the Lord," bold Moses said;
    Let my people go,
If not I'll smite your first born dead,
    Let my people go.

Go down, Moses,
    'Way down in Egypt land,
Tell ole Pharaoh,
    To let my people go.[19]

The constantly recurring refrain, "Let my people go," is typical of the prayers of lamentation. Repetition is of the essence of lamentation. The significance of this is something that far exceeds poetry. Nor is it explained by ethnic culture. One does not have to be black to enter into this supplication. One of the things that makes it universal is its typology. Whites understand the imagery as well as blacks. In fact, a great amount of the prayer of the spirituals is typological. "I look'd over Jordan, an' what did I see? . . . A band of angels comin' after me."[20] Such prayers obviously transcend the merely ethnic; they are clearly universal, and the typology helps make them universal. But, even more than the typology, what makes them universal is that they express the common longing of all peoples for redemption. It is this that glorifies the God of our salvation, and it is this, therefore, that makes them worship.

19. James Weldon Johnson and J. Rosamond Johnson, *The Book of American Negro Spirituals* (New York: Viking Press, 1940), pp. 51-53.

20. Johnson and Johnson, *The Book of American Negro Spirituals,* pp. 62-63.

# III

## Kerygmatic Doxology

Let us speak now of a kerygmatic doxology. By *kerygmatic doxology* we mean worship as proclamation. It was not until New Testament times that biblical worship became kerygmatic in the most proper sense, but the beginnings of kerygmatic doxology are found in the acclamations of the Temple. Proclamation begins with acclamation. The most popular acclamation of the Temple was "Hallelujah."[1] Another was, "The LORD reigns," as we find it in Psalms 93, 97, and 99. And still another was that festive shout, "O give thanks to the LORD for he is good; for his steadfast love endures forever," found as a sort of antiphon in Psalms 105, 106, 107, 118, and 136. The song of the seraphim heard by Isaiah, "Holy, holy, holy is the LORD of hosts; the whole earth is full of his glory" (6:3) is surely to be understood as an acclamation. Like the acclamations that greeted the arrival of an earthly king, these liturgical acclamations greeted the presence of the heavenly sovereign.

The essential point of an acclamation is that it recognizes the presence of an august personage. It is an expression of

---

1. On the liturgical acclamations of Temple, church, and synagogue, see Eric Werner, *The Sacred Bridge: Liturgical Parallels in Synagogue and Early Church* (New York: Schocken Books, 1970).

41

awe and wonder. It is the appropriate reaction to majesty. At the same time that an acclamation recognizes the presence of the ruler, it recognizes that ruler's sovereignty. When worshipers in the Temple shouted "The LORD reigns," they were recognizing not only that God was uniquely present to the worshiping congregation but also that he was present as the one who had authority over that congregation.

Acclamation is at the core of the biblical concept of praise. In fact, it is so basic to the concept of praise that one could say that all the hymns of praise found in the Bible spring from that basic acclamation, "Hallelujah." Many of the psalms were chanted with "Hallelujah" as a constantly recurring refrain. Indeed, the worship of the Temple reverberated with this acclamation. A good commentary on the meaning of *Hallelujah* is found in Psalms 146–50, the last five psalms of the Psalter.[2] These hymns of praise are but an unfolding of this basic acclamation. In Psalm 146 it is the individual soul that recognizes God's sovereign grace to the humble and by this recognition is inspired to sing this acclamation:

Praise the LORD!
  Praise the LORD, O my soul!
I will praise the LORD as long as I live;
  I will sing praises to my God while I have being. . . .

Happy is he whose help is the God of Jacob,
  whose hope is in the LORD his God,
who made heaven and earth,
  the sea, and all that is in them;
who keeps faith for ever;
  who executes justice for the oppressed;
  who gives food to the hungry.

2. See Hans-Joachim Kraus, *Psalmen,* 2d ed., 2 vols. in *Biblischer Kommentar altes Testament,* vol. 15 (Neukirchen: Neukirchener Verlag, 1961), 2: 968.

The LORD sets the prisoners free;
   the LORD opens the eyes of the blind.
The LORD lifts up those who are bowed down;
   the LORD loves the righteous.
The LORD watches over the sojourners,
   he upholds the widow and the fatherless;
   but the way of the wicked he brings to ruin.

(Vv. 1-2, 5-9)

This is an acclamation to God as the savior of those in need, particularly of those who in some personal need had called on God for deliverance and in that deliverance had found that their God was indeed their savior.

In Psalm 147 it is Jerusalem that acclaims the sovereignty of God in gathering the outcasts of Israel and filling the land with the finest of the wheat:

Praise the LORD!
For it is good to sing praises to our God;
   for he is gracious, and a song of praise is seemly.
The LORD builds up Jerusalem;
   he gathers the outcasts of Israel. . . .

Praise the LORD, O Jerusalem!
   Praise your God, O Zion!
For he strengthens the bars of your gates;
   he blesses your sons within you.
He makes peace in your borders;
   he fills you with the finest of the wheat.

(Vv. 1-2, 12-14)

Here it is the unfathomable grace of election that brings God's people to wonderment. How is it that God has chosen us? This we can never understand; all we can do is acclaim his electing grace.

In Psalm 148 the sovereignty of God is discovered over

43

the host of heaven, the sun, the moon, and all the shining stars, sea monsters and all deeps, fruit trees and all cedars. When one is confronted by the vastness of creation, what can one do but be overwhelmed with awe and acclaim God as Creator?

In Psalm 149 God's triumphal sovereignty on the day of judgment is envisioned. As Hans-Joachim Kraus has so aptly put it, the faithful of Israel praise the Lord that even though they were powerless in this world, they will be raised in the last day by the sovereign grace of God to participate in the final judgment of the world.[3] Here it is the mystery of the Last Day, the eschaton, that incites the worshiper to an awe-filled Hallelujah!

Finally, in Psalm 150 God's sovereignty is recognized in the worship of the sanctuary, where trumpet, harp, and pipe acclaim God's presence.

> Praise the LORD!
> Praise God in his sanctuary;
>     praise him in his mighty firmament!
> Praise him for his mighty deeds;
>     praise him according to his exceeding greatness!
>
> Praise him with trumpet sound;
>     praise him with lute and harp!
> Praise him with timbrel and dance;
>     praise him with strings and pipe!
> Praise him with sounding cymbals;
>     praise him with loud clashing cymbals!
> Let everything that breathes praise the LORD!
> Praise the LORD!

There have been those who have understood these formulas of praise as "calls to worship" rather than worship

---

3. On the relation of the concept of praise and the recognition of God's claim on the Gentiles, see Kraus, *Psalmen,* 2: 798.

itself. But there is more to it than that. The praises of the Psalter are indeed formulas of praise directed to God, but many of these formulas are marked by what might be called a reverent indirection. It belonged to oriental court etiquette that one addressed the king indirectly. This would explain the fact that few of the hymns of praise found in the Psalter address God in the second-person singular. Other psalm genres address God in the second-person singular — the votive thanksgiving psalms and the lamentations, for example — but it is different with the hymns of praise. It was somewhat the same way as it is today in Germany, where it is considered a mark of respect to address someone in the third-person plural — that is, indirectly. Yet while these acclamations are far more than calls to worship, they do envision, almost prophetically, that all nations, even the Gentiles, will recognize the kingdom of God. Psalm 97 begins, "The LORD reigns; let the earth rejoice; let the many coastlands be glad!" and then continues, "The heavens proclaim his righteousness; and all the peoples behold his glory" (vv. 1, 6). If God is to be acclaimed as Lord of all the earth, then it is fitting that all the peoples of the earth not only behold his glory but acclaim his reign.

In fact, Psalms 95–100 form a cluster that insist on the universality of God.

> O come, let us sing to the LORD;
>> let us make a joyful noise to the rock of our salvation!
> Let us come into his presence with thanksgiving;
>> let us make a joyful noise to him with songs of praise!
> For the LORD is a great God,
>> and a great King above all gods.
> In his hand are the depths of the earth;
>> the heights of the mountains are his also.
> The sea is his, for he made it;
>> for his hands formed the dry land. (Ps. 95:1-5)

45

That he is God over all nature implies that he is God over all mere gods or godlings. If God is to be king, then he must be king over the spiritual as well as the temporal spheres of life. This is drawn out even further in Psalm 99:

> The LORD reigns; let the peoples tremble!
>> He sits enthroned upon the cherubim; let the earth quake!
> The LORD is great in Zion;
>> he is exalted over all the peoples.
> Let them praise thy great and terrible name!
>> Holy is he!
> Mighty King, lover of justice,
>> thou hast established equity;
> thou hast executed justice
>> and righteousness in Jacob.
> Extol the LORD our God;
>> worship at his footstool!
>> Holy is he! (Vv. 1-5)

When prayed through from beginning to end, this cluster of psalms is nothing less than a hymnic development of the evangelistic imperative, and yet in no part of the Bible is the praise of God's people developed more richly. Finally these prayers come to a mighty conclusion.

> Make a joyful noise to the LORD, all the lands!
>> Serve the LORD with gladness!
>> Come into his presence with singing!·

> Know that the LORD is God!
>> It is he that made us, and we are his;
>> we are his people, and the sheep of his pasture.

> Enter his gates with thanksgiving,
>> and his courts with praise!
>> Give thanks to him, bless his name!

For the LORD is good;
  his steadfast love endures for ever,
  and his faithfulness to all generations. (Ps. 100)

What a mighty affirmation of the universality of God!

Psalm 117, although it is the shortest hymn in the Psalter, expresses the central thrust of the biblical concept of praise.

Praise the LORD, all nations!
  Extol him, all peoples!
For great is his steadfast love toward us;
  and the faithfulness of the LORD endures for ever.
Praise the LORD!

The hymn both begins and ends with the acclamation "Hallelujah." This introductory and concluding acclamation affirms the presence of the God who is enthroned on the praises of Israel and who is revealed in steadfast love and faithfulness. Even when Moses received the theophany on Mt. Sinai, he did not see the face of God but rather "The LORD passed before him, and proclaimed, 'The LORD, the LORD, a God merciful and gracious, slow to anger, and abounding in steadfast love and faithfulness . . .'" (Exod. 34:6). The acclamation of God's presence included the naming of the divine attributes of steadfast love and faithfulness. To experience the presence of God was not to see God's face but to experience the graciousness, the steadfast love, and the faithfulness of God. Essential to the biblical hymns is the acclamation that God's praise endures forever. It was only natural, as we find here in Psalm 117, that this acclamation of God's eternity would be complemented by an acclamation of God's universality. The God who is acclaimed by all ages is surely to be praised by all peoples. Already in the worship of the Temple, acclamation moves to proclamation. Praise must eventually become evangelism.

With Jesus the acclamations of the Temple became the

47

proclamation of the gospel. The preaching ministry of Jesus proclaimed that the kingdom of God is at hand.[4] We read in the Gospel of Mark that Jesus came, preaching the gospel of God: "The time is fulfilled, and the kingdom of God is at hand" (1:15). His preaching fulfilled the acclamation of the Temple, "The LORD reigns." The preaching of Jesus and the apostles was basically doxological, as it proclaimed the reign of God and claimed the faithfulness of all peoples to that reign, so that the universal praise of all peoples envisioned by the praises of the Temple was fulfilled.

Quite consistently the New Testament uses a very specific word to designate the preaching of the gospel. This preaching is referred to as being *kerygma* —that is, "proclamation." Again we have a word connected with the court. *Kerygma* was the proclamation of a herald who announced the presence of a royal personage or proclaimed the king's rule or his decrees. It belonged to the royal dignity that the king's word was proclaimed by a herald, a minister of the king's glory. In the same way, the New Testament church understood the preacher of the gospel as serving the glory of her Lord.

One might distinguish between acclamation and proclamation by saying that in acclamation one accepts for oneself that Christ is Lord, while proclamation is a witness to others that Christ is Lord. When Jesus preached in the synagogue of Nazareth, he chose as his text a passage from Isaiah that made quite clear what he meant by proclamation.

"The Spirit of the Lord is upon me,
because he has anointed me to preach good news to the poor.

4. Gerhard Friedrich quite correctly makes the point that in the ministries of both Jesus and his apostles, the preaching of the Word implies the presence of the Word. Through preaching, the Son of God is actively present ("κῆρυξ . . . ," *Theological Dictionary of the New Testament,* ed. Gerhard Kittel and Gerhard Friedrich, trans. Geoffrey W. Bromiley, 9 vols. [Grand Rapids: William B. Eerdmans, 1964-1974], 3: 683-718).

He has sent me to proclaim release to the captives
and recovering of sight to the blind,
to set at liberty those who are oppressed,
to proclaim the acceptable year of the Lord."

(Luke 4:18-19)

One notices two things here. First, there is the proclamation of the coming messianic king, the announcement of the acceptable year of the Lord. Second, there is the proclamation of the good news that this coming of the messianic king brings with it the care of the poor, the release of captives, the healing of the blind, and liberty for the oppressed. As the concept of proclamation developed in the New Testament era, the apostles came to be understood as heralds of Christ and his resurrection. We find this idea with particular clarity in Paul's account of his preaching ministry to the Corinthians (1 Cor. 15:1-2). He had proclaimed that Christ was raised from the dead to the glory of the Father. We find much the same thing in 1 Peter, where the proclamation of the mighty acts of salvation is part of the spiritual service of the royal priesthood (2:9). As Philippe Menoud points out, the proclamation of the gospel as Paul understands it is particularly directed toward the non-Christian world.[5] It is noteworthy that the ultimate fulfillment of praise in the worship of the heavenly Jerusalem is the acclamation "Worthy is the Lamb who was slain" (Rev. 5:12). The word *axios,* "worthy," was used in the Greek-speaking world to acclaim a ruler. The worship of heaven is preeminently acclamation as the great multitudes of vic-

---

5. See Menoud, *L'Eglise et les ministéres selon le Nouveau Testament* (Neuchâtel: Delachaux et Niestlé, 1949). A good summary of Menoud's work is found in his article "Preaching," in *The Interpreter's Dictionary of the Bible,* 5 vols., ed. George A. Buttrick and Keith R. Crim (Nashville: Abingdon Press, 1962-1975), 3: 868. See also K. Goldammer, "Der Kerygmabegriff in der ältesten christlichen Literatur," *Zeitschrift für die neuentestamentliche Wissenschaft* 48 (1957): 77-101; and Friedrich, *Theological Dictionary of the New Testament,* 3: 683-718.

torious saints cry out "Hallelujah! For the Lord our God the Almighty reigns" (19:6). This worship is clearly the ultimate unfolding of the Hallelujah psalms as well as Psalms 93, 97, and 99, which acclaim the reign of God over all peoples for all eternity.[6]

Given the importance of acclamations in the worship of the heavenly Jerusalem as we find it in the book of Revelation, one can hardly be surprised to discover acclamations in the earliest records we have of Christian worship. The *Didache* reports the use of both *Hosanna* and *Maranatha* as acclamations in the celebration of the Lord's Supper. In both cases they are jubilant cries recognizing the presence of the long-awaited Messiah. This is even more obvious when we notice that Hosanna has been joined with Psalm 118:26, "Hosanna, blessed be he that cometh in the name of the Lord" (KJV).[7] This acclamation, filled with messianic sentiments, was shouted by the crowds of Jerusalem when Jesus entered the city at the beginning of his Passion. As used by the early church, it was an acclamation of messianic fulfillment.

At an early point in the history of Christian worship, these acclamations evolved into hymns. The most obvious example of this is the *Gloria,* the oldest Christian hymn that has come down to us:

> Glory be to God on high:
>> and on earth peace,
>> good will towards men.

> We praise Thee,
>> we bless thee,
>> we worship thee,

6. For a full discussion of this, see my article "The Psalms of Praise in the Worship of the New Testament Church," *Interpretation* 39 (1985): 20-33.

7. Cf. Werner, *The Sacred Bridge,* pp. 263ff.

we glorify thee,
we give thanks to thee for thy great glory.

O Lord God, heavenly King:
God the Father Almighty.

O Lord, the only begotten Son,
Jesus Christ:
O Lord God,
Lamb of God,
Son of the Father

That takest away the sins of the world:
have mercy upon us.

Thou that takest away the sins of the world:
Receive our prayer.

Thou that sittest at the right hand of the Father:
have mercy upon us

For Thou only art holy:
Thou only art the Lord.

Thou only, O Christ, with the Holy Ghost:
art most high in the glory of God the Father.

One notices first of all that this hymn is an elaboration of
the acclamation of the angels recorded in the Gospel of Luke.
The heavenly herald proclaims the appearance of the Savior,
who "is born this day in the city of David" (2:11). The proclamation is accompanied by an appropriate acclamation as the
heavenly host sings, "Glory to God in the highest" (v. 14).
This oldest of Christian hymns is an elaboration of the acclamation of the angels. It recognizes God as heavenly King
and Jesus as the Christ, the Son of the Father, the only Son.
The fact that Christ is recognized as the only begotten, the

*monogenes,* is significant.[8] What that probably meant to the ancient church was that Jesus was recognized, in royal terminology, as the prince, the heir of divine power.[9] A royal acclamation was therefore appropriate. It is the acclamation of a congregation that knows Christ not only as God but as Lamb of God and therefore Savior of the world.

In the Byzantine liturgy the singing of *Tris Hagion* is one of the high points of the service. This, too, is a biblical acclamation that has been elaborated into a hymn.[10]

Holy God, Holy Mighty, Holy Immortal,
  Have mercy upon us.
  Glory be to the Father and to the Son and to the
    Holy Ghost.

Holy God, Holy Mighty, Holy Immortal,
  Have mercy upon us.
  From everlasting to everlasting, world without end.

Holy God, Holy Mighty, Holy Immortal,
  Have mercy upon us.

With both the *Gloria* and the *Tris Hagion,* the parallels with the acclamations used in the imperial court are striking. The worship of the Eastern Orthodox churches makes much use

8. On the correct translation of *monogenes,* see F. Büchsel, "μονογενής," in *Theological Dictionary of the New Testament,* 4: 737-41; and D. Moodey, "God's Only Son," *Journal of Biblical Literature* 72 (1953): 72.

9. On the evolution of this ancient text from the acclamation of the angels found in the Gospel of Luke and of the christological titles found in it, see B. Capelle, "Le texte du *'Gloria in excelsis,'*" in *Travaux Liturgique,* 3 vols. (Louvain: Centre liturgique, 1962), 2: 176-91; and J. A. Jungmann, *Missarum Sollemnia. Eine genetische Erklärung der römischen Messe,* 5th ed., 2 vols. (Freiburg: Herder, 1962), 1: 446-61.

10. On acclamations as a source of hymnody, see Egon Wellescz, *Byzantine Music and Hymnography* (Oxford: Clarendon Press, 1962), pp. 98-122.

of courtly rhetoric. In fact, the whole Byzantine liturgy could be understood as one long, richly developed acclamation. This is particularly the case with its superb hymnology.[11]

It is Ambrose of Milan who is usually credited with introducing hymnody into the Latin church. The hymnody he introduced had a strong element of acclamation. This is quite obvious from his well-known morning hymn:

> O Splendor of God's glory bright,
> From light eternal bringing light,
> Thou Light of light, light's living Spring,
> True Day, all days illumining:
>
> Come very Sun of heaven's love,
> In lasting radiance from above,
> And pour the Holy Spirit's ray
> On all we think or do today.
>
> And now to thee our prayers ascend,
> O Father, glorious without end;
> We plead with Sovereign Grace for pow'r
> To conquer in temptation's hour.
>
> Confirm our will to do the right,
> And keep our hearts from envy's blight;
> Let faith her eager fires renew,
> And hate the false, and love the true.
>
> O joyful be the passing day
> With thoughts as pure as morning's ray
> With faith like noontide shining bright,
> Our souls unshadowed by the night.

---

11. See Wellescz, *Byzantine Music,* pp. 98-122. Cf. Hans Joachim Schulz, *The Byzantine Liturgy* (New York: Pueblo Publishing, 1986), pp. 22-25; and H. Engberding, "Zum formgeschichtliche Verständnis des Trishagions," *Jahrbuch für Liturgiewissenschaft* 10 (1930): 168-74.

Dawn's glory gilds the earth and skies,
Let him, our perfect Morn, arise,
The Word in God the Father one,
The Father imaged in the Son.[12]

One of the aspects of acclamation that comes out with particular clarity in this as well as in other Ambrosian hymns is that of submission to divine authority. The rising of the sun becomes the occasion for recognizing the appearance of the Son of God as the true source and authority of human life. It is the recognition of this authority that enlightens human life. At the beginning of the day, Christ is greeted as the Light of light, the splendor of God's glory. The appearance of God's Son makes possible the illumination and purification of the faithful. He is therefore acclaimed as the source of moral order and perfection, and the acclamation is therefore quite logically followed by a prayer for sanctification. Acclamations were not without their moral implications. An acclamation is quite practically a moral imperative. If Christ really is king, the anointed of the Lord, then surely his will is to be obeyed and his way is to be followed.

The evangelistic aspect of acclamation is especially clear in another Ambrosian hymn, "Savior of the Nations, Come."

Saviour of the nations, come,
Virgin's Son, make here thy home!
Marvel now, O heav'n and earth,
That the Lord chose such a birth.

Not of flesh and blood the Son,
Offspring of the Holy One;
Born of Mary ever blest
God in flesh is manifest.

12. On the authenticity of this hymn, see A. S. Walpole, *Early Latin Hymns* (Cambridge: Cambridge University Press, 1922), pp. 35-39. The English translation is by Louis F. Benson.

Wondrous birth! O wondrous Child
Of the virgin undefiled!
Though by all the world disowned,
Still to be in heav'n enthroned.

From the Father forth he came
And returneth to the same,
Captive leading death and hell,
High the song of triumph swell!

Thou, the Father's only Son,
Hast o'er sin the vict'ry won.
Boundless shall thy kingdom be;
When shall we its glories see?

Praise to God the Father sing,
Praise to God the Son, our King,
Praise to God the Spirit be
Ever and eternally.

The hymn as it now stands is a proclamation of Christ as the Savior of the Gentiles who by his wondrous birth is now revealed to the nations as their Redeemer.[13] As Redeemer of the nations, Christ has conquered sin and death and therefore is acclaimed as victor, the rightful ruler of a great kingdom.

The kerygmatic thrust of early Christian hymnody had its obvious complement in the pulpit. Some of the greatest patristic preaching can be understood in terms of acclamation. One thinks immediately of the *Theological Orations* of Gregory of Nazianzus.[14] This series of six sermons heralded the orthodox

13. Originally, the first stanza began by acknowledging Christ as Shepherd of Israel, but during the Middle Ages the first stanza dropped out. The text provided here is Catherine Winkworth's translation of Luther's *Nun komm, der Heiden Heiland.* Cf. Walpole, *Early Latin Hymns,* pp. 50-57.

14. On the preaching of Gregory of Nazianzus, see Rosemary Radford Ruether, *Gregory of Nazianzus: Rhetor and Philosopher* (Oxford: Claren-

doctrine of the person of Christ in the city of Constantinople at a time when the church in Constantinople, and in fact much of the East, had gone over to Arianism. In A.D. 379, Gregory was sent to Constantinople to be pastor of the Orthodox minority in the city. The archbishop was of strong Arian sympathy and was not too happy with Gregory's presence. In effect, Gregory was an Orthodox missionary in Arian territory, and his six sermons were in effect missionary sermons. They constitute a carefully reasoned presentation of orthodox christology. Preached in the high rhetorical style so popular in the period, they were received by the people of Constantinople with enthusiasm. In classical antiquity oratory was a popular art form. Champion orators enjoyed the same popularity as champion athletes, and Gregory of Nazianzus was a champion orator. For centuries the Byzantine church has regarded Gregory's sermons as classics of Christian oratory. Somehow the elegant rhetoric increases the festal sense of these proclamations. The language of the preacher intimates the august character of the personage proclaimed. Gregory of Nazianzus, with his gift for elegant oratory, was for the city of Constantinople the best possible herald of the gospel.

That preaching belongs to the kerygmatic dimension of worship hardly needs belaboring. One can find many examples all the way through the history of Christian worship of great evangelists whose preaching, like that of Gregory of Nazianzus, was thoroughly doxological. The centrality of this insight for the Protestant Reformation is axiomatic. Luther, Zwingli, and Calvin all put the proclamation of the gospel at the center of worship. This we all know, but I would now like to turn to a point that is less well known.

Surely one of the most beautiful variations of the keryg-

---

don Press, 1969); and J. Bernardi, *La prédication des pères cappodociens, le prédicateur et son auditoire* (Paris: Presses Universitaires de France, 1968).

matic theme is the liturgical music of German Protestantism, especially its organ music.[15] Here is one of the glories of Protestant worship! It is in the context of the kerygmatic doxology that one can best appreciate the origins of instrumental music in Christian worship. The stylized acclamations of the oriental court had a definite place for instrumental music.[16] Again, in the empires of antiquity, it was with horns and trumpets that the arrival of the sovereign was heralded. It was the same way with the emissaries of the king who were sent to represent his person. Then, too, fanfares from musical instruments regularly signaled royal proclamations. We find that in the Temple of Jerusalem they proclaimed feast days as well (Ps. 81:3). Even in the synagogue the beginning of the Sabbath was announced by the blowing of the shofar. On the other hand, the early Christian church used no musical instruments in worship.[17] It was not until the reign of Charlemagne that organs began to be introduced into churches, and only after that did other instruments appear. To this day most Eastern Orthodox churches do not allow musical instruments. Be that as it may, instrumental music became a regular part of Christian worship in Western Europe during the Middle Ages.

In the seventeenth and eighteenth centuries organ music came to full flower in Germany. Its function was clearly kerygmatic, just as the music of the Temple had been. Johann Pachelbel at the Lorenzkirche in Nuremberg, Dietrich Buxte-

---

15. A large amount of literature has been produced on the subject of German Protestant church music. A particularly comprehensive collection is found in *Leiturgia. Handbuch des evangelischen Gottesdienstes,* 5 vols., ed. Karl Ferdinand Müller and Walter Blankenburg (Kassel: Johannes Stauda, 1961). The fourth volume is dedicated to the subject of liturgical music.

16. See Wellescz, *Byzantine Music,* pp. 105-9.

17. See Johannes Quasten, *Musik und Gesang in den kulten der heidnischen Antike und christlichen Frühzeit* (Münster in Westphalia: Aschendorf, 1930), pp. 166-72.

hude at the Marienkirche in Lübeck, and Johann Sebastian Bach at the Thomaskirche in Leipzig provided Protestant worship with a collection of magnificent musical settings. The organ preludes and postludes gave the whole service the air of a festive acclamation of God's presence. The spirit of this music is kerygmatic. Today when a service of worship begins with Bach's Toccata and Fugue in D Minor, one is aroused to hear the proclamation of the gospel. It is the function of preludes to claim our attention for a momentous event. In the same way, it is the function of a postlude to affirm the surpassing importance of the worship that has just been celebrated.[18]

At the time of Bach's death, his younger contemporary Charles Wesley had already composed some of his most memorable hymns, striking examples of the vitality of acclamation in Christian doxology. To be fully appreciated, however, they must be seen as the complement of evangelistic preaching. The hymnody of the evangelical revival that was springing up all over in those days served with the preaching to produce a joyful, exultant sort of worship. Wesley's hymns are at the same time both acclamation and proclamation.

> Ye servants of God, your Master proclaim,
> And publish abroad His wonderful Name;
> The Name, all victorious, of Jesus extol;
> His Kingdom is glorious, and rules over all.

> God ruleth on high, almighty to save;
> And still He is nigh — His presence we have:
> The great congregation His triumph shall sing,
> Ascribing salvation to Jesus, our King.

---

18. On the function of organ music in worship, see Hans Klotz, "Die kirchliche Orgelkunst," *Leiturgia,* 4: 759-803; Christhard Mahrenholz, *Orgel und Liturgie* (Kassel, 1928); and Hans-Joachim Moser, *Die evangelische Kirchenmusik in Deutschland* (Berlin, 1954). See particularly the chapter "Orgel und Orgelspiel" in Gotthold Frotscher's *Geschichte des Orgelspiels und der Orgelkomposition,* 2 vols. (Berlin, 1959).

Salvation to God who sits on the throne!
Let all cry aloud and honor the Son:
The praises of Jesus the angels proclaim,
Fall down on their faces and worship the Lamb.[19]

Obviously Wesley thought out the meaning of Christian praise in great depth. Christian praise is both a continuation of the praise of the Temple and an anticipation of the praise of the heavenly Jerusalem. Note how the word *salvation* has become an acclamation: "Salvation to God who sits on the throne!" This hymn has both a strong sense of the majesty of God and a clear recognition of the presence of God: "God ruleth on high, almighty to save; And still He is nigh — His presence we have." Proclamation rejoices in presence, a point stressed in another of Wesley's hymns:

Rejoice the Lord is King:
Your Lord and King adore!
Rejoice, give thanks, and sing,
And triumph ever more:
Lift up your heart, lift up your voice!
Rejoice, again I say, rejoice![20]

When acclamation and proclamation are held together as closely as the Wesleys held them together, preaching — even evangelistic preaching — is thoroughly doxological.

The emphasis of much eighteenth- and nineteenth-century preaching was overwhelmingly kerygmatic. During the reign of Queen Victoria, England had a whole constellation of evangelical preachers, particularly among the Baptists and Congregationalists. Charles Haddon Spurgeon was the outstanding preacher of the age, but Alexander Maclaren and Joseph

19. Charles Wesley, *Hymns for Times of Trouble and Persecution*, vol. 1 (London: Strahan, 1744), p. 43.
20. Charles Wesley, *Hymns for our Lord's Resurrection* (London: W. Strahan, 1746), #8.

Parker were extraordinarily gifted preachers as well.[21] Significantly, these men democratized the proclamation of the gospel. It was not that they ignored the biblical imagery of king and kingdom so much as they realized there was more to God's glory than any earthly king or queen had ever reflected. For them the majesty of the cross and the splendor of the resurrection outshone by far the pomp and circumstance of even the British Empire. Most of these men were of humble origins and realized the necessity of taking the gospel in all its fullness to the common people. They understood God's glory to be served in the simple obedience of the Christian life far more than in pageantry.

Spurgeon lacked a formal theological education.[22] Before he was twenty years old he became a Baptist preacher. It was almost as a child prodigy that he built a rather humdrum London chapel into the Metropolitan Tabernacle, seating some five thousand people. Child prodigies often fade in older years, but Spurgeon engaged in intense study of Scripture and the vast literature of seventeenth-century Puritanism, amassing an astounding biblical and theological knowledge. Without professors or classroom lectures, he studied the classics of theological literature and thereby gained a deep understanding of the essence of the Christian gospel. He tells us in *Lectures to My Students* that he was always concerned in his preaching to proclaim Christ, to announce the gospel to those who had never quite heard it. In this concern he was typical of a whole age of preaching.

In our grandparents' generation, the hymns of Fanny

21. On preaching in Victorian England, see Horton Davies, *Worship and Theology in England from Newman to Martineau, 1850-1900* (Princeton, N.J.: Princeton University Press, 1962), especially pp. 282-348.

22. A particularly interesting study of Spurgeon has been given to us by the distinguished German theologian and preacher Helmut Thielicke — *Encounter with Spurgeon,* trans. John W. Doberstein (Philadelphia: Fortress Press, 1963).

Crosby expressed the piety of America. Anyone who has ever seen the little Southeast Presbyterian Church out in the country not far from Pawling, New York, where Fanny Crosby went to church in her childhood will have a sense of the simple and solid kind of doxology that our ancestors really had.[23] One of her most popular hymns is a perfect acclamation:

> Praise him! praise him! Jesus, our blessed Redeemer!
> Sing, O earth, his wonderful love proclaim!
> Hail him! hail him! highest archangels in glory;
> Strength and honor give to his holy Name!
> Like a shepherd, Jesus will guard his children,
> In his arms he carries them all day long:
> Praise him! praise him! tell of his excellent greatness;
> Praise him! praise him! ever in joyful song!
>
> Praise him! praise him! Jesus, our blessed Redeemer!
> For our sins he suffered, and bled, and died;
> He our Rock, our hope of eternal salvation,
> Hail him! hail him! Jesus the Crucified.
> Sound his praises! Jesus who bore our sorrows,
> Love unbounded, wonderful, deep and strong:
> Praise him! praise him! tell of his excellent greatness;
> Praise him! praise him! ever in joyful song!
>
> Praise him! praise him! Jesus, our blessed Redeemer!
> Heav'nly portals loud with hosannas ring!
> Jesus, Saviour, reigneth for ever and ever;
> Crown him! crown him! Prophet, and Priest, and King!
> Christ is coming! over the world victorious,
> Pow'r and glory unto the Lord belong:
> Praise him! praise him! tell of his excellent greatness;
> Praise him! praise him! ever in joyful song!

23. For a recent work on the liturgical significance of Fanny Crosby, see Keith Watkins, "A Few Kind Words for Fanny Crosby," *Worship* 51 (1977): 248-59.

Here we find all the rhetoric of the court, just as we find it in the Psalms and the patristic hymns. Christ is to be crowned. He is indeed prophet, priest, and king. He is coming to be victorious over the world, and to him belong power and glory. Yet, somehow, in Fanny Crosby's hymn the court rhetoric seems to fade before the proclamation of the wonderful love of Jesus, who is king, yes, but a shepherd-king, the crucified, love unbounded. This hymn, primitive as it may be, is filled with the classic affirmation of kerygmatic doxology. It is American folk liturgy at its best!

# IV

## Wisdom Doxology

One of the major contributions of recent biblical scholarship has been the delineation of the Wisdom theology, the scholastic theology of the Jews. It developed particularly among the scholars who were responsible for preserving the tradition of the Hebrew Scriptures. It was these learned scribes who produced the handwritten manuscripts of the Torah with a sort of devotion that won them high respect. These scribes were the sages of Israel. Their chief concern was to preserve the books of the Law and the oracles of the prophets, but they also produced a considerable literature of their own. They loved to collect proverbs, wise sayings, and liturgical texts from the past. In time their own writings and their collections of writings came to be regarded as Scripture. The Wisdom theology was still very much alive in the days of Jesus and the apostles. It had a strong influence on the New Testament, particularly on the Epistle of James and the Gospel of John. It came to full flower in the logos theology of the early church.

The Wisdom theology inspired some very distinctive attitudes toward worship. It is this that I would like to call the *Wisdom doxology*. Although liturgical scholars have not yet taken up on it, Gerhard von Rad's *Wisdom in Israel* has a major contribution to make to our understanding of wor-

63

ship.[1] The Wisdom theology was scholarly, meditative, and moral. Its approach to doxology, therefore, encouraged a disciplined study of the Scriptures as the revelation of the divine Wisdom that enlightens all human life. The Wisdom doxology is summarized by that line from the first Psalm, "his delight is in the law of the LORD, and on his law he meditates day and night" (Ps. 1:2). The divine Wisdom was the glory of God, and wherever the Scriptures were studied and taught that Wisdom shone forth and God was glorified.

The profound theologian who put Psalm 19 into its canonical form expressed the Wisdom doxology very well.

> The heavens are telling the glory of God;
> and the firmament proclaims his handiwork.
> Day to day pours forth speech,
> and night to night declares knowledge.
> There is no speech, nor are there words;
> their voice is not heard;
> yet their voice goes out through all the earth,
> and their words to the end of the world. . . .
>
> The law of the LORD is perfect,
> reviving the soul; . . .
> the precepts of the LORD are right,
> rejoicing the heart; . . .
> the ordinances of the LORD are true,
> and righteous altogether. (Vv. 1-4, 7-9)

The divine Wisdom that orders the heavens glorifies God. The same divine Wisdom revealed in the Law perfects the soul, makes wise the simple, and rejoices the heart. This, too, glorifies God. When God's Word orders human life, God is glorified. God's Word is God's greatest glory. It is a radiant transforming glory that brings order to the creation. The study

---

1. Von Rad, *Wisdom in Israel*, trans. James D. Martin (Nashville: Abingdon Press, 1972).

of the Law is worship just as is the awe-filled wonder of beholding a starry night or a glowing sunset.

Wherever the insights of the Wisdom school are cherished, Psalm 119 usually appears as a particularly beloved passage of Scripture. It expresses many of the fondest thoughts of the sapiential books of the Old Testament. Psalm 119 shows us how the study of the Law was worship for the scholars of the Wisdom school. They prayed, "Open my eyes, that I may behold wondrous things out of thy law" (v. 18). They studied the Scriptures that they might behold the Wisdom that is the divine glory. They memorized the Scriptures that their lives might glorify God. "I have laid up thy word in my heart, that I might not sin against thee" (v. 11). Daily they studied the Scriptures that God's Word might direct all their actions. "Thy word is a lamp to my feet and a light to my path" (v. 105). The glory of God was a sanctifying glory, a glory that enlightened the darkness of life, drove out sin, and established righteousness. The glory of God made the life of God's people glorious. When God's people reflect his glory, then God is glorified.

In the Song of Solomon we find another aspect of the Wisdom doxology. In the opinion of most of today's biblical scholars, the Song of Solomon began as a collection of songs used at wedding celebrations. Originally they had no religious significance, but in time Jewish piety began to find an analogy between the delight and devotion that bride and groom have for each other and the delight and devotion that the godly have for sacred Wisdom. They delight in the Law of the Lord day and night. Whatever the Song of Solomon may originally have meant, by New Testament times it was fairly common to understand this poetry as a hymn to the divine Wisdom.[2] For

---

2. On the early history of the Christian interpretation of the Song of Solomon and its roots in the interpretation of the Jewish synagogue, see von Rad, *Wisdom in Israel,* pp. 166-76; and O. Rousseau, *Origène. Homélies sur le Cantique des Cantiques* (Paris: Éditions du Cerf, 1966), pp. 7-57.

the sages of Israel, devotion to the divine Wisdom was a sacred passion.

The Gospel of John marks an important development of the Wisdom theology.[3] John interprets the divine Wisdom as the *logos,* the Word. "In the beginning was the Word, and the Word was with God, and the Word was God. . . . In him was life, and the life was the light of men. The light shines in the darkness, and the darkness has not overcome it" (John 1:1, 4-5). Here John is drawing on an idea that sometimes appears in Jewish speculative thought, that the divine Wisdom was the first of God's creations. Proverbs 8:30 speaks of the divine Wisdom being with God in creation: "then I was beside him, like a master workman; and I was daily his delight, rejoicing before him always." John goes beyond Proverbs, to be sure, first in discovering that the divine Wisdom is God and second in identifying the divine Wisdom with Christ. Christ is the Word, the holy light, enlightening the faithful and delighting the Father. This idea found in Proverbs 8:30, that the divine Wisdom delights God, is important for worship. If the Word, the divine Wisdom, delights God, "rejoicing before him always," then its place in worship is easily understandable. "Word" may be a Greek philosophical term, but it translates a thoroughly Hebrew concept. "And the Word became flesh and dwelt among us, full of grace and truth; we have beheld his glory, glory as of the only Son from the Father" (John 1:14). When this key text is understood from the standpoint of Jewish Wisdom theology rather than Greek philosophy, then we understand that the incarnate truth is the very glory of God and the glory of God is a gracious glory that transforms human life, and when the Word transforms human life, then God is glorified.

3. On the importance of Wisdom motifs in the Gospel of John, see Raymond E. Brown, *The Gospel according to John I–XII,* Anchor Bible Series (Garden City, N.Y.: Doubleday, 1966), pp. 122-25.

The influence of the Wisdom school on the Gospel of John is made particularly clear by the story of the wedding feast at Cana found in the second chapter. There Jesus is revealed as the true bridegroom who turns the purifying water of the Law into the wine of the gospel. The nuptial theme must have been important in the teaching of Jesus, for we find it reappearing in several of his parables, such as the parable of the wise and foolish virgins and the parable of the wedding feast of the king's son. It was the influence of the Wisdom school that led the New Testament church to understand worship as a foretaste of what the Revelation calls the wedding feast of the Lamb.

In early Christian Wisdom theology, the affirmation that Christ is the Word did not replace the idea that the study of Scripture is in itself worship. Quite the contrary: it intensified it and opened the way to regarding the writings of the apostles as Scripture. In the reading and preaching of the Scriptures, God was to be encountered. "These are written that you may believe that Jesus is the Christ, the Son of God, and that believing you may have life in his name" (John 20:31). The life-giving logos could be discovered in the written Scriptures. The written Gospel presented Christ to be believed. It was not as though in the incarnation the book was replaced by a person; rather, by the reading and preaching of the Scriptures, Christ, the Word, was recognized as being truly present. "Blessed are those who have not seen and yet believe" (20:29). John believed every bit as much as Paul that faith comes by hearing. Wisdom theology gives a high priority to the exposition of Scripture in public worship.

The Wisdom doxology gives an equally important place to the sacrament of the Lord's Supper. This is intimated in the Johannine literature, where, as Raymond Brown has shown, the Wisdom motifs and the sacramental motifs are closely connected.[4] In the story of the wedding feast, Christ reveals

4. Brown, *The Gospel according to John I–XII*, pp. 272-74.

himself to be the true bridegroom of the Song of Solomon by providing the wine that the bridegroom of Cana failed to provide. In the story of the feeding of the multitude, Christ presents himself as the true bread that comes down from heaven and gives life to the world. He is the divine Wisdom, and when the faithful receive his teaching, then, as Isaiah had promised, they are taught by God (John 6:45). The Christian feeds on the true bread by faith and receives eternal life. There have always been those who have understood the Gospel of John to be speaking of the preaching of Jesus and nothing more, but then there are those, like Oscar Cullmann, who would insist that what is said concerns not only the Word but the Supper as well.[5] It is from this line of thought that one comes to understand the Supper as the Word made visible, and participation in it as a covenantal union with the Word. "He who eats my flesh and drinks my blood abides in me, and I in him" (6:56). When John speaks of the marriage supper of the Lamb in Revelation 19:9, the relation of Wisdom motifs and eucharistic motifs is made very clear. The Supper is communion with the incarnate Word, who died and has risen and lives evermore.

The *Odes of Solomon* is a treasury of early Christian doxology brimming with implications for the theology of worship.[6] One must study the whole collection of hymns to get the feel of its unique imagery. We will need to take a good long look at this oldest of Christian hymnals, but even at that we will only make a beginning. The *Odes of Solomon* are Syriac poetry that at first reading seems rather exotic, but they

5. See Cullmann, *Early Christian Worship*, trans. A. Stewart Todd and James B. Torrance (Philadelphia: Westminster Press, 1978), pp. 93-102.

6. *Odes of Solomon*, ed. and trans. James Hamilton Charlesworth (Chico, Calif.: Scholars Press, 1977). All subsequent quotations will be taken from this edition. For more detailed commentary, see J. Rendel Harris and Alphonse Mingana, *The Odes and Psalms of Solomon*, 2 vols. (Manchester: John Rylands Library, 1916-1920).

maintain a continuity with the Semitic lyrical tradition. They are Christian psalms, a Christian continuation of the psalmic tradition. Nowhere else in the literature of the ancient church do we get such a feeling for Christian love, for the joy of justification by faith, or for the sheer delight of praise. Praise is a ministry! It is an important service to God. Christian hymnody, according to the *Odes of Solomon,* is the fulfillment of the Song of Solomon. The ministry of praise is worship at its most intimate. It is the outpouring of the love of the church for the divine Wisdom incarnate in Christ.

> My art and my service are in His hymns,
> Because His love has nourished my heart,
> And His fruits He poured unto my lips.
>
> For my love is the Lord;
> Hence I will sing unto Him.
>
> For I am strengthened by His praises,
> And I have faith in Him.
>
> I will open my mouth,
> And His spirit will speak through me
> The glory of the Lord and His beauty. . . . (Ode XVI, 2-5)

Christian praise is the outpouring of the love with which Christ has filled the hearts of the faithful. It is the Word that produced the praise that on the lips of the church now glorifies the Word. It is the same way with Christian preaching.

> He has filled me with words of truth,
> That I may proclaim Him.
>
> And like the flowing of waters, truth flows from my
>     mouth,
> And my lips declare His fruits.

And He has caused His knowledge to abound in me,
Because the mouth of the Lord is the true Word,
And the entrance of His light.

And the Most High has given Him to His generations,
(Which are) the interpreters of His beauty,
    And the narrators of His glory,
    And the confessors of His purpose,
    And the preachers of His mind,
    And the teachers of His works. . . .

For the mouth of the Most High spoke to them,
And His exposition prospered through Him.

For the dwelling place of the Word is man,
And His truth is love.

Blessed are they who by means of Him have perceived
    everything,
And have known the Lord in His truth.
    Hallelujah. (Ode XII, 1-13)

The preaching of the Word glorifies God because it is the outpouring of the truth that God has poured into the hearts of Christian preachers. Preaching glorifies God because it is the preaching of his Word. God delights in the Word, and God is therefore worshiped in its being preached and its being heard.

God delights in the preaching of the Word because it is his Word, but also because this preaching, like all worship, is the work of his Spirit. Worship as we find it in the *Odes of Solomon* has a trinitarian dynamic to it. It originates in the sacred communion between the persons of the Trinity. Worship is the work of the Holy Spirit. This comes out with particular clarity in Ode VI:

As the wind moves through the harp
And the strings speak,

So the Spirit of the Lord speaks through my members,
And I speak through His love. . . .

The Lord has multiplied His knowledge,
And He was zealous that those things should be known
which through His grace have been given to us.

And His praise He gave us on account of His name;
Our spirits praise His Holy Spirit. (Ode VI, 1-7)

The ministry of praise arises from the activity of the Holy
Spirit, who moves the hearts of Christians in their service of
praise. God's Spirit gives us his praises, and therefore our
spirits praise God through his Holy Spirit. In worship, as we
find it in the *Odes of Solomon,* the faithful are drawn into the
communion of the Father, the Son, and the Holy Spirit.

Ode VIII shows us another dimension of worship. The
ministry of the Word belongs to the spiritual sacrifice. I will
have more to say about the spiritual sacrifice later, but here I
must say something about it from the perspective of the Wisdom school. The hymn begins,

Open, open your hearts to the exultation of the Lord,
And let your love abound from the heart to the lips.

In order to bring forth fruits to the Lord, a holy life;
And to talk with watchfulness in His light. (Ode VIII, 1-2)

The author, as was common for early Christians, understands
Christian worship as the sacrifice of praise offered by the
righteous. This is a basic principle of New Testament liturgical
theology. We find in the Epistle to the Hebrews, for example,
that worship is the continual "sacrifice of praise to God, that is,
the fruit of lips that acknowledge his name" (13:15). The *Odes
of Solomon* often speak of the fruits presented to the Lord, by
which is meant the sacrifice of praise. For early Christians who

71

had set aside the worship of the Temple with its ceremony and its sacrifices, there was an important affirmation of their understanding of worship in the prophecy of Hosea (14:2). Hosea looked for the day when Israel would repent of her wickedness and render to the Lord the fruit of her lips which was the true sacrifice. The people of God must pass beyond the rituals of sacrifice and present offerings of the heart, praise and prayer, works of righteousness and mercy, for in the end these are the sacrifices that please God. In the Wisdom theology, especially, these sacrifices of the heart were understood to include right understanding and pure teaching of the truth. This is surely what we are to understand by the phrase "and to talk with watchfulness in His light." To preach pure doctrine, to hear such preaching and add one's "Amen" to it, is understood as worship. Preaching belongs to the spiritual sacrifices of the royal priesthood along with praise and prayer. This is made very clear, as the ode says, *ex ore Christi,*

> Hear the word of truth,
> And receive the knowledge of the Most High. . . .
>
> And understand my knowledge, you who know me in
>     truth;
> Love me with affection, you who love. (Ode VIII, 8-11)

Again we note that worship is a divine work. Here it is preaching rather than praise that God brings about in Christian worship. God himself teaches through the ministry of the Word. It is of the very nature of the relation between the Creator and the creature that the God who makes us teaches us. As it is understood by the Wisdom theology, God's grace illumines the minds that his fingers have fashioned. This same idea is found in the Gospel of John. It is by his Word that God creates and by that same Word that he illumines. In this hymn the odist uses yet another image, the image of the mother who both forms the child and nourishes the child:

72

I fashioned their members,
And my own breasts I prepared for them,
That they might drink my holy milk and live by it.

(Ode VIII, 14)

All through the *Odes of Solomon* it is clear that the ministry of the Word is at the center of Christian worship.

The Wisdom doxology of the *Odes of Solomon* is just as eloquent on the subject of the sacraments of baptism and the Lord's Supper as it is on the Word. Ode XI begins with a striking typological image of baptism.

My heart was pruned and its flower appeared,
Then grace sprang up in it,
And it produced fruits for the Lord.

For the Most High circumcised me by His Holy Spirit,
Then He uncovered my inward being towards Him,
And filled me with His love. (Ode XI, 1-3)

This obvious reference to baptism is followed by references to tasting living water. This no doubt has implications for the eucharist as well as for the ministry of the Word.

And speaking waters touched my lips
From the fountain of the Lord generously.

And so I drank and became intoxicated,
From the living water that does not die.

And my intoxication was not with ignorance;
But I abandoned vanity,

And turned towards the Most High, my God,
And was enriched by His favors. (Ode XI, 6-9)

As the ode progresses, the eucharistic implications become more clear. The theme of the sacred meal is taken up again.

73

This Christian psalm, according to Rendel Harris, is a development of Psalm 36:7-9, which tells us that God's people "feast on the abundance of thy house, and thou givest them drink from the river of thy delights. For with thee is the fountain of life; in thy light do we see light." This psalm lends itself very naturally to the insights of early Christian Wisdom theology. The odist has interpreted Psalm 36 with the help of the Song of Solomon. The feast of which the psalm speaks is the wedding feast in the garden of Solomon with all its exotic fragrances, its fruitful trees, its choice fruits, and its fountain of living water.

> My eyes were enlightened,
> And my face received the dew;
>
> And my breath was refreshed
> By the pleasant fragrance of the Lord.
>
> And He took me to His paradise,
> Wherein is the wealth of the Lord's pleasure. . . .
>
> Then I worshipped the Lord because of His magnificence.
>
> And I said, Blessed, O Lord, are they
> Who are planted in Thy land,
> And who have a place in Thy Paradise. (Ode XI, 14-16)

The garden is Paradise, Paradise seen from the Song of Solomon. It is the Paradise in which the marriage feast of the Lamb takes place. But the wedding feast is also the feast at Cana. A number of the themes of the story of turning water into wine appear in this ode. First we hear of the water from the rock and then we hear of the holy inebriation that comes from this water. All this, of course, is the standard imagery of early Christian Wisdom theology. It was already understood to have eucharistic implications when we find it in the Gospel parable

74

of the wedding feast of the king's son and when the Revelation of John tells us of the blessedness of those who are invited to the wedding feast of the Lamb. The eucharistic theology of the *Odes of Solomon* has a strong eschatological dimension. According to the *Odes of Solomon,* to partake of the Lord's Supper is to taste in this life the life of the world to come. The Supper is a foretaste and a promise of our eternal communion with God.

These Christian psalms are surely among the most lyrical developments of Christian doxology. They do not give us a *systematic* theology of worship, to be sure, but they do give us a theology of worship. Perhaps one could call it a biblical theology of worship. It abounds in types, and perhaps for this reason it does not quite fit into systematics. But maybe that is simply the nature of doxology.

One of the most important developments of the Wisdom doxology is found in the work of Origen. A native of the city of Alexandria and teacher of the Christian catechetical school, Origen was a natural heir to the logos philosophy the Jewish theologians and neo-Platonic philosophers of Egypt had developed in the three centuries immediately preceding him. Alexandria was a city with an imposing cultural heritage, and Origen was intent on interpreting the Scriptures to the most enlightened spirits of his day. The Wisdom theology of the Old Testament had a number of obvious points of contact with the learned culture of Alexandria. Alexandria was a city devoted to books and book culture; it had the largest library of the ancient world.

As a preacher, Origen was first of all interested in the interpretation of Scripture. This was quite natural for someone who had been so deeply influenced by the Wisdom school. Today we usually find Origen of interest because of what made him unusual — his allegorical interpretation of the Scriptures. A generation ago these interpretations were commonly viewed as ridiculous or, at best, amusing, but today we are beginning to realize that there is an amazing wisdom in them, almost in spite of the allegories.[7] Beyond this, there are many ways in which Origen was representative of his age. He is the first Christian preacher from whom we have any significant number of sermons, and in many ways his approach to preaching was typical of Christian preaching in the first three centuries. This is most obviously the case with his great interest in the exposition of Scripture. The earliest Christian preachers were fascinated by finding Christ in the Old Testament, just as Origen was. In the second century the church and the synagogue were still in close contact with each other. In such cities as Caesarea and Alexandria, Christian preachers had to show that Jesus was the fulfillment of the Law and the Prophets if they were going to have any evangelistic impact at all. Christian preachers of the first three Christian centuries were all influenced by the Wisdom school and by the logos theology even if they did not draw from it the same methods of exposition or the same philosophical conclusions Origen did.

Origen's preaching ministry was extensive. During his years in Caesarea Philippi (231–ca. 254) he preached his way through most of the books of the Bible. These sermons were taken down by stenographers and kept in the library of the church of Caesarea. If it had not been for the theological vicissitudes of following centuries, we would have had expository sermons from that genius of exposition for almost the whole Bible. But during the sixth century, under the reign of Justinian, there was a strong reaction against Origen and a systematic attempt to destroy his work. Some of it, providen-

7. The work of Jean Daniélou and his students has done much to retrieve this genius of the ancient church. Cardinal Daniélou's extraordinary book *Origène* (Paris: La table ronde, 1948) is a classic. See also Pierre Nautin, *Origène. Sa vie et son ouvre* (Paris: Beauchesne, 1977). On the Christian culture of Alexandria, see Robert L. Wilken, *Judaism and the Early Christian Mind: A Study of Cyril of Alexandria's Exegesis and Theology* (New Haven: Yale University Press, 1971).

tially, has been preserved. We have large numbers of his sermons on the historical books of the Old Testament; we have his sermons on the Gospel of Luke and on the Epistle to the Romans. Although, with a few exceptions, we do not have them in the original Greek, we do have them in translation, and this is sufficient to give us a clear picture of his preaching ministry. It was a significant life work and a memorable intellectual accomplishment which the church remembered for a long time. The point that needs to be made is that there must have been many less-well-known preachers who preached along the same lines in those days. To be sure, they would not have evidenced the brilliance of Origen's white-hot fire of genius, but simply because the biblical Wisdom tradition was so strong, we can safely assume that these more obscure preachers would have given the same careful attention to the regular and systematic interpretation of Scripture. This whole school of early Christian thought understood the study of Scripture in the assembly of God's people to be worship at its most faithful.

With the end of classical civilization, learning fell on hard days, and it is easy to understand how the Wisdom school would have found it difficult to survive. Nevertheless, there were those who devoted themselves to the preservation of sacred learning. Dom Jean Leclercq in his book *The Love of Learning and the Desire for God* has shown us how the concerns of the Wisdom theology were expressed in the ministry of the Word maintained by medieval monasticism.[8] The monks devoted themselves to book culture in much the same way the sages of Israel had. Theirs was a comprehensive book culture that included not only the study and preaching of the Scriptures but the collection of biblical manuscripts and tradi-

---

8. Leclercq, *The Love of Learning and the Desire for God: A Study of Monastic Culture,* trans. Catharine Misrahi (New York: Fordham University Press, 1961).

77

tions of interpretation as well. It included copying these manuscripts and guarding their accuracy. Like the sages of Israel before them, the monks developed a very studious piety. As Leclercq has pointed out in his various studies, the preaching of Bernard of Clairvaux is a flowering of this literary piety. The sermons of Bernard are hymns of love to the incarnate Word of God. His remarkable series of sermons on the Song of Solomon is indeed the monastic *summa theologica,* but it is also a renaissance of the Wisdom doxology.

At the time of the Protestant Reformation, the Wisdom theology underwent a thorough reevaluation. The Reformers, being students of Christian Humanism, were naturally inclined to favor the highly literary piety of Origen, but on the other hand they did not like his approach to exegesis.[9] They preferred the grammatical-historical approach of the Antiochene school to the allegorical approach of the Alexandrian school. Yet the Reformers did approve of Origen's approach to the ministry of the Word. Melanchthon, in particular, voiced much sympathy with Origen in this regard. The piety of the Reformers took on more and more of a literary cast as they pored over the Scriptures day by day. The study of the Wisdom books of the Old Testament received new attention from the Reformers, and the Wisdom doxology reappeared with considerable vigor.

The first liturgical reform that all of the Reformers made was the establishment of regular expository preaching. This was true of Luther, of Zwingli, of Brenz, of Bucer, of Calvin, and even of Knox. Regular expository preaching was usually established even before there was any change in the worship service, even before the liturgy was translated into the common language. The ministry of Ulrich Zwingli is exemplary

9. On the sixteenth-century evaluation of Origen, see my *Patristic Roots of Reformed Worship* (Zurich: TVZ, 1975), p. 178. For a more recent study, see Max Schär, *Das Nachleben des Origenes im Zeitalter des Humanismus* (Basel: Helbing & Lichtenhahn, 1979).

in this regard. In 1519, when Zwingli was called to the Great Minster in Zurich, he decided to begin his work there by preaching through the Gospel of Matthew chapter by chapter, verse by verse. This he did daily, and every able-bodied man and woman in Zurich turned out to hear him. The second year he did the same thing with the Gospel of John. Then he took up the Acts of the Apostles, the Epistle to the Hebrews, the First Epistle of Peter, and the Pauline Epistles. In his first five years he preached through most of the New Testament. Then he turned to the Old Testament, studying the Hebrew text with all the new methods of literary science developed by the Renaissance. For more than a decade prior to his years in Zurich he had prepared for this ministry with an intensive study of Scripture in the original languages. He even copied out the Greek text of the New Testament in his own hand, meticulously noting the textual variations in the margin as he read through the writings of the Church Fathers. Zwingli was a bookworm in much the same way that the ancient rabbis of the Wisdom school had been, in much the same way as Origen had been. In those earliest years of his ministry, as pastor of Glarus way up in the Alps where he was snowbound for months at a time, Zwingli collected an amazing library. It was particularly strong in biblical commentaries. He had all the commentaries on sacred Scripture by Chrysostom, Jerome, and Augustine that the printing presses of the Christian Humanists were beginning to make available. He was devoted to the study of the sacred page, and it was with this devoted learning that he won the hearts of the Christian population of Zurich.

A rather surprising place where the Wisdom doxology makes an appearance is in the eucharistic doctrine of John Calvin. As will become clear further on, there are other important elements of Calvin's eucharistic doctrine, but when he begins to follow Augustine's doctrine of the sacrament as *verbum visibile,* the visible Word of God, Calvin's sapiential approach to the sacraments begins to appear.[10] The sacraments, as Calvin understands it, are the signs and seals by which the Word of God is confirmed. This implies, of course, the full and highly developed sense of the Word of God found in the Wisdom tradition. The Word is more than just words of instruction, more than just law: it is the Word full of grace and truth, the divine Wisdom. It is the Word in the sense of the term developed by the Wisdom school that becomes visible in the sacrament. For Calvin the doctrine of the *verbum visibile* does not say that the sacrament is the teaching of Christian doctrine through pantomime or some such thing as much as it insists that the eternal Word who has become flesh in the person of Jesus Christ is to be encountered in the worship of the Christian church, in the reading and preaching of Scripture, in the sharing of the loaf and the cup.

Particularly in relation to the Lord's Supper, Calvin likes to speak of the Word as communicating life to those who receive it in faith. At considerable length he develops his understanding of the Johannine logos theology as it relates to the Lord's Supper.

> Christ was from the beginning that life-giving Word of the Father [John 1:1], the spring and source of life, from which all things have always received their capacity to live. Therefore, John sometimes calls him, "the Word of life" [I John 1:1], sometimes writes that "in him was life" [John 1:4].[11]

Calvin develops this thought in order to explain the bread-of-life discourse in the sixth chapter of John. The Word of God, like the manna that came down from heaven, is a heavenly food. When the Word of God is truly preached and rightly believed, it is a heavenly feast, a sacred banquet

---

10. See Calvin, *Institutes of the Christian Religion,* 4.14.4.
11. Calvin, *Institutes,* 4.17.8.

shared with God himself. Going on with his interpretation of the Gospel of John, Calvin speaks of the incarnation or manifestation of the Word in the flesh, Jesus Christ. This was to the end that

> he also quickens our very flesh in which he abides, that by partaking of him we may be fed unto immortality. "I am," he says, "the bread of life come down from heaven. And the bread which I shall give is my flesh, which I shall give for the life of the world." [John 6:48, 51; cf. ch. 6:51-52, Vg.] By these words he teaches not only that he is life since he is the eternal Word of God, who came down from heaven to us, but also that by coming down he poured that power upon the flesh which he took in order that from it participation in life might flow unto us.[12]

It is from the incarnate Christ, crucified and risen, that believers receive new and eternal life. It is from him that they are born into this new and eternal life and from him that they are nourished by this new and eternal life. This life is both represented to us and bestowed upon us in the sacraments.

> Now, that sacred partaking of his flesh and blood, by which Christ pours his life into us, as if it penetrated into our bones and marrow, he also testifies and seals in the Supper — not by presenting a vain and empty sign, but by manifesting there the effectiveness of his Spirit to fulfill what he promises. And truly he offers and shows the reality there signified to all who sit at that spiritual banquet, although it is received with benefit by believers alone, who accept such great generosity with true faith and gratefulness of heart.[13]

Calvin's eucharistic theology is covenantal in that it understands that in the Lord's Supper we are united to Christ. It

12. Calvin, *Institutes,* 4.17.8.
13. Calvin, *Institutes,* 4.17.10.

is also sapiential in that Calvin believes that the Christ to whom we are united is the Word of life who makes us alive with eternal life. The Word has a creative vivifying power. When it is believed, it transforms human life and makes it holy. Calvin believes in the eucharistic presence of the ascended Christ through the work of the Holy Spirit who dwells within us. That indwelling presence transforms us so that more and more we bear the image of Christ. When God's people reflect his image, then he is magnified and his abiding presence is manifested in the world. Just as it is the Holy Spirit who makes the preaching of the Word effective in our lives, so it is the Holy Spirit who makes Christ present in the sacrament to those who believe, and to them the Word is a living, sanctifying presence, the Word of grace and truth. The eucharistic presence of the Word is manifest when it is received by faith and lived in holiness. To stop short of this is to truncate the whole Christian experience of worship.

Calvin's doctrine of the real presence has often been called vitalistic, or dynamistic. But it is not some philosophy of vitalism or dynamism that is at play here; rather, it is the Wisdom theology of the Gospel of John. It is the comprehensive understanding of what the Word of God really is that Calvin got from the Wisdom writers of the Old Testament and from the Gospel of John. The Wisdom doxology as it is expressed in Calvin's doctrine of the eucharistic presence emphasizes that it is the Word who is present. He is present through the work of the Holy Spirit both in the preaching of the gospel and in the hearing of it in faith. He is present when God's people reflect his holiness.

The Wisdom doxology was expressed in the Protestant pulpit for generations to come. Valerius Herberger (1562-1627) was preacher to a small German-speaking city in the province of Silesia in the far eastern region of Germany along the Polish border. The area suffered greatly during the Thirty Years War. For most of Herberger's ministry his city was under a Catholic prince, and he found himself ministering to a church in a hostile environment. He has long been regarded as one of the great preachers of Lutheran orthodoxy. Following the example of Martin Luther, he preached thoroughly expository sermons. On Sunday he would expound the required pericopes of the Lutheran lectionary. During the week he preached through individual books of the Bible one after another. In the course of his ministry he preached through almost the entire Bible. His Old Testament sermons, published and widely circulated throughout Germany, were particularly beloved. These sermons, typical of the period, show a high appreciation for the biblical narrative in itself. The preacher is obviously interested in what the text has to say. For Herberger, the passage of Scripture never becomes a mere starting point for a discussion of some theological doctrine or moral teaching. He was inclined to preach on longer passages rather than single verses, since this helped him to keep closer to the original scope of the biblical authors. His expositions convey a warm and virile piety. The Word, true to the Wisdom tradition, was a Word of life.

It is from the standpoint of the Wisdom doxology that we best understand the preaching of Protestant orthodoxy. Johannes Cocceius (1603-1669) in seventeenth-century Netherlands, Jean Daillé (1594-1670) in Paris, and Thomas Manton (1620-1677) in Puritan London all exhibited a great devotion to explaining the text of Scripture. Let us not imagine that the faithful found sermons an hour or two long to be tedious. To the contrary, they loved them. In 1662, when Charles II restored the monarchy and ejected the Puritans from their churches, Manton continued to preach wherever he could. His hearers risked fine and imprisonment to hear him carefully explain the text of the Bible verse by verse, chapter after chapter. Manton's 190 sermons on the 119th Psalm represent what must be the most thorough and careful study of a passage of Scripture that any preacher has ever attempted. The whole series is permeated with a sense of the wonder of God's Word.

Both the preacher who preached these sermons and the congregation which listened knew that God was to be encountered in the preaching of the Word, and that is why they happily gave it the time, hour upon hour.

The devotion to the sacred text typical of the Wisdom doxology helps us to understand much Christian choral music. It was because the text was sacred, because it was so respected and beloved, that it was sung. It is the great love for Scripture that helps us to understand particularly the choral music of Heinrich Schütz.[14] While still a boy, Schütz began his musical career as a singer in the chapel of the Prince of Hesse. The Prince of Hesse had traditionally leaned rather heavily toward Reformed Protestantism. The singing of the Psalms occupied a privileged place in the worship of the Reformed church. It is not surprising, therefore, that throughout his life the Psalms played a cardinal role in the doxology of Heinrich Schütz. He did two large series of psalm settings, one earlier and the other later in his career.[15] In addition to this, he provided the Becker Psalter with musical settings that even today are quite popular.[16]

As his musical career advanced, Schütz spent time in

14. On the music of Schütz, see Walter Blankenburg, "Der mehrstimmige Gesang und die konzertierende Musik," in *Leiturgia. Handbuch des evangelischen Gottesdienstes,* vol. 4, ed. Karl Ferdinand Müller and Walter Blankenburg (Kassel: Johannes Stauda, 1961), pp. 662-718; F. Blume, "Heinrich Schütz in den geistigen Strömungen seiner zeit," *Musik und Kirche* 2 (1930): 245-54; H. J. Moser, *Die mehrstimmige Vertonung des Evangeliums* (Leipzig, 1931); and H. J. Moser, *Heinrich Schütz: His Life and Work,* trans. C. F. Pfatteicher (St. Louis, 1959).

15. *Psalmen Davids* appeared in 1619. These psalms were produced for the chapel of the Duke of Saxony and show the strong influence of the Italian baroque style. The psalms that appeared in the *Symphoniae sacrae,* part II (1647) and part III (1650) are of a much simpler nature.

16. This psalter is made up of ninety psalms put into German meter by the Leipzig theologian Cornelius Becker. It was published in 1628. A series of modern adaptations of these psalms is available from Concordia Publishing House in St. Louis.

Venice studying under Gabrieli at the gold-domed Cathedral of St. Mark. There his music took on the grandeur of the Italian baroque style. Returning north, he occupied the position of music director at the court of the Duke of Saxony, one of the most prestigious princes of Germany. There he produced the traditional choral pieces of the Lutheran liturgy. He wrote motets for the Gospels and Epistles of the lectionary, magnificats for vespers, and passions for Holy Week. Particularly remarkable are his *Kleine geistliche Konzerte,* musical settings for individual texts of Scripture. No one has ever done a more superb job of setting Scripture to music. Each text of Scripture is set in music like a precious stone mounted in a ring. What one always hears is the text; what one always remembers is the sacred Word.

As Schütz grew older, his music became much simpler. His *Passion according to St. John* of 1665 is so simple that every word of the sacred text is distinctly heard. It is the text of Scripture that is emphasized. Schütz lived to a considerable age, and in the later years his devotion to the Holy Bible increased to the point that it was the only book he read. Hour upon hour he searched its pages. His final series of psalm settings is amazingly simple. It has the simplicity of utter genius, a total devotion to the Word of God. His setting of Psalm 119, the longest of the psalms and a psalm particularly remarkable in its reflection of the spirit of the Wisdom school, is the work of an old man whose delight, all his life, had been in the Law of the Lord in which he had meditated day and night.

Among the Puritans of England and New England and among the Presbyterians of Scotland, Ireland, and the American Middle Colonies, one begins to hear another variation to the Wisdom theme of Christian doxology. More and more one finds that worship is understood in terms of the nuptial imagery of the Song of Solomon. It is the feast of heavenly Wisdom mentioned in the ninth chapter of Proverbs, the wed-

85

ding feast of the king's son mentioned in the parable of Jesus, and the marriage supper of the Lamb in the Revelation. Early in the seventeenth century the Puritans began to develop a rich doctrine of Christian love in their expositions of the Song of Solomon. Richard Sibbes and John Cotton both published extensive series of sermons on this book. In America, Thomas Shepard preached his memorable series of sermons *The Parable of the Wise and Foolish Virgins.* This work, almost mystical in character, virtually launched American theology. It was a great inspiration to Jonathan Edwards, David Brainerd, and many of the leaders of the Great Awakening. In this work Shepard explains worship as the communion between the Bridegroom and the Bride. Preaching is the word of love that wins the heart of the Bride. The office of the ministry of the Word is to press the suit of the Bridegroom. It is to woo for Christ.[17]

John Willison, a minister in the Scottish city of Dundee in the first half of the eighteenth century, wrote a considerable amount of material on worship. One finds, predictably, a very strong covenantal theology of worship in Willison's works. I will have more to say about this further on, but here I want to note the way the Wisdom doxology unfolded in his eucharistic doctrine. This is especially evident where he makes a particular point of speaking of the eucharist in the imagery of the Song of Solomon. At the sacrament, Christ brings us into his banqueting house and his banner over us is love (Song of Sol. 3:4). Here is Christ's gracious presence and here is the sight of his presence (3:3). As another Scotsman put it, "Here, O my Lord, I see thee face to face."[18] The Lord's Supper is

17. See *The Parable of the Wise and Foolish Virgins,* in vol. 1 of *The Works of Thomas Shepard* (Boston, 1857), p. 41.

18. Horatius Bonar (1808-1889) was the most prolific hymnodist of nineteenth-century Scotland. In 1883 he served as Moderator of the Free Church. The communion hymn mentioned here is a fair statement of traditional Scottish eucharistic piety.

the sacrament of Christ's presence and therefore a joyful feast, a wedding feast.[19]

Gilbert Tennent (1703-1764), who began his pastoral career with the Presbyterian Church in New Brunswick, New Jersey, was one of the leaders of the Great Awakening.[20] In later years he was called to Second Presbyterian Church in Philadelphia. A recently discovered collection of his manuscript sermons preserved in the archives of Princeton Seminary's Speer Library shows how important the Song of Solomon and related passages of both the Old and New Testaments were to the development of Tennent's theology of the love of God.[21] Tennent viewed the celebration of the Lord's Supper as an expression of the love between Christians and Christ. At the Lord's Supper it was, therefore, particularly appropriate to preach on Christ's love to us and our love to Christ. One of the sermons in this collection that was apparently preached at the Lord's Supper is based on the parable of the wedding feast of the king's son in Matthew 22:1-14. Covenantal theology is strong in the sermon, but so is Wisdom theology. It is in the manifestation of God's compassionate love that the glory of God is revealed. God is served when the invitation to the wedding feast is presented to us and we come to the feast. This, of course, is an evangelistic sermon, but, when understood in the context of the Wisdom theology, the doxological nature of the sermon is patent. God is worshiped when we come to the wedding banquet and rejoice in the feast that is spread before us. God is worshiped when we love him because he first loved us.

19. See John Willison, *The Practical Works,* ed. W. M. Hetherington (London: Blackie & Son, [ca. 1830]), pp. 303-9.

20. For a particularly fine study of the ministry of Gilbert Tennent, see Milton J. Coalter, Jr., *Gilbert Tennent, Son of Thunder: A Case Study of Continental Pietism's Impact on the First Great Awakening in the Middle Colonies* (Westport, Conn.: Greenwood Press, 1986).

21. See my article "Gilbert Tennent and the Preaching of Piety in Colonial America," *Princeton Seminary Bulletin* 10 (1989): 132-37.

It is not surprising that Mary Lathbury, an American who devoted her life to producing Bible study materials for the Methodist Sunday School Union, should have given us a hymn that voices the Wisdom doxology:

Break thou the bread of life,
Dear Lord, to me,
As thou didst break the loaves
Beside the sea;
Throughout the sacred page
I seek thee, Lord,
My spirit pants for thee,
O living Word.

Bless thou the truth, dear Lord,
To me, to me,
As thou didst bless the bread
By Galilee;
Then shall all bondage cease,
All fetters fall;
And I shall find my peace,
My All in all.

Thou art the Bread of Life,
O Lord, to me,
Thy holy Word the truth
That saveth me;
Give me to eat and live
With thee above;
Teach me to love thy truth,
For thou art love.

O send thy Spirit, Lord,
Now unto me,
That he may touch mine eyes,
And make me see:

Show me the truth concealed
Within thy Word,
And in thy Book revealed
I see the Lord.[22]

What makes this hymn so interesting is that it shows us the other side of the *verbum visibile* coin. If the Supper is a visible Word, then the teaching of the Word is a holy feast through which we enter into communion with God.

22. Mary A. Lathbury, "Break Thou the Bread of Life," *The Church School Hymnal for Youth* (Philadelphia: Westminster Press, 1938), #157. For another version of the text, see Mary A. Lathbury, *Poems* (Minneapolis: Nunc Licet Press, 1915).

# V

# Prophetic Doxology

The fourth type of doxology I would like to outline is the *prophetic doxology*. The key to the prophetic doxology is that the holiness of God demands the holiness of his people. The holiness of God is magnified when it is reflected by a holy people. This is what the second commandment is about. God's people are the proper image of God and the most significant reflection of God's glory. Neither gold nor silver nor stone can reflect the righteousness, the faithfulness, or the loving-kindness of God. Refined gold might serve as a simile of holiness, but God will not view adoration of an image of even the purest gold as acceptable worship. What God asks of us is the love of a pure heart, the well-ordered devotion of a righteous and just people. The prophet Micah put it very simply: "What does the LORD require of you but to do justice, and to love kindness, and to walk humbly with your God?" (6:8).

The first commandment has to do with love for God. It demands our undivided love, the kind of wholehearted, single-minded love that is the essence of both monogamy and mono-theism. Such love is exclusive. It tolerates neither indifference nor ambiguity. The love of God for us is jealous; it disdains the dispassionate and the dilettante. What the love of God will have from us is a sacred passion. Jesus taught that it is this

91

kind of love that is demanded by the first and greatest commandment — love with all our hearts, all our minds, and all our souls. It is from this kind of love that holiness springs. Holiness is wholehearted devotion to God and his ways. It is holiness that is the subject of the second commandment. It teaches us that the love we offer to God must be sincere; it must be whole and unadulterated. It insists that we be holy, that we ourselves be the faithful image of God, rather than fashioning vain images of wood or stone, silver or gold.

The worship experience of Isaiah in the Temple was a revelation of the holiness of God. "Holy, holy, holy is the LORD of hosts; the whole earth is full of his glory" (Isa. 6:3). This was the acclamation of the seraphim, but it was also the demand of the Torah: "You shall be holy; for I the LORD your God am holy" (Lev. 19:2). Isaiah responds to it by confessing that he is a sinner and that he dwells in the midst of sinners. But in this experience of worship Isaiah is purified with a glowing coal from the altar. His sin is forgiven and he is sent to preach holiness to his people. The holiness of God will judge Judah with fire, but in the burnt stump is the holy seed. Isaiah's worship was an experience of God's urgent demand for holiness. He himself was purified in that worship that he might serve the holiness of God. The holy God will have a holy people.

The prophets were critical of the worship of their day because it was adopting the idolatry and the elaborate ceremonial of the Canaanites. J. L. Mays expresses it in modern idiom very well: the cult had been Canaanized.[1] As the prophets saw it, idolatry was to be rejected because God had forbidden it, and even the forms of worship that God had commanded must be performed with sincerity of heart and integrity of life.

1. Mays, *Micah: A Commentary* (Philadelphia: Westminster Press, 1976), p. 45.

"I hate, I despise your feasts,
　　and I take no delight in your solemn assemblies.
Even though you offer me your burnt offerings and
　　cereal offerings,
　I will not accept them,
and the peace offerings of your fatted beasts
　I will not look upon.
Take away from me the noise of your songs;
　　to the melody of your harps I will not listen.
But let justice roll down like waters,
　　and righteousness like an ever-flowing stream."

(Amos 5:21-24)

Amos was not opposed to services of worship.[2] He was opposed to worship that was insincere, that served the pride of the worshipers, their love for the theatrical and the luxurious, but neglected God's demand for holiness. No matter how profound the symbolism of the rites or how beautiful the music, they had usurped the primary concerns of worship. Such things had taken the place of communion with God. The more the ceremonial had been elaborated, the more the teaching of the Law had been neglected. Even worse, immorality on the part of those who worshiped obscured the holiness of God. The worship of the wicked confuses, even contradicts, the revelation of God's presence. Justice and righteousness are essential to the worship God will have from Israel, for it is in the justice and righteousness of his people that the glory of God is magnified. Justice, honesty, and morality are essen-

---

2. The extent of the prophet's criticism of the worship of the Temple has been discussed at length. For a short review of the discussion, see Masao Sekine, "Das Problem der Kultpolemik bei den Propheten," *Evangelische Theologie* 28 (1968): 605-9. Particularly helpful are the following: H. W. Hertzberg, "Die prophetische Kritik am Kult," *Theologische Literaturzeitung* 75 (1950): 219-26; and Th. Chary, *Les prophets et le cult à partir de l'Exil* (Paris: Desclèe, 1955).

tial to the integrity of worship. They are not the same thing as worship, and certainly they are not more important than worship, but without them there is no true worship.

Righteousness was an essential concept for the prophets. Righteousness meant being in right relationships. Right relationships demanded justice, truthfulness, chastity, generosity, humility, courage, industriousness, and whatever virtues were appropriate to the different positions one occupied in society. To be righteous, one must be honest in business, truthful in court, faithful to one's wife or husband, and generous to the poor. There was a whole complex of right relationships involved here: right relationships with God, with the family, with the neighbor, with one's own people, and even with foreigners. One could not be righteous if one had right relationships with God but not with one's family or one's neighbor. Amos maintained that true worship demands righteousness, which is to say that it demands the whole complex of right relationships.

The prophetic approach to doxology is an important constituent of the New Testament's theology of worship just as it is of the Old Testament's.[3] Jesus himself was very critical of the worship conducted in both synagogue and Temple. We find this in the Sermon on the Mount (6:1-18).[4] There Jesus stresses that what God will have above all else from us is not the outward forms of prayer, fasting, and almsgiving but

3. A number of contemporary scholars have shown that in taking up the prophets' criticism of worship, the New Testament does not spiritualize worship. See J. Behm, "θύω . . . ," in *Theological Dictionary of the New Testament*, ed. Gerhard Kittel and Gerhard Friedrich, trans. Geoffrey W. Bromiley, 9 vols. (Grand Rapids: William B. Eerdmans, 1964-1974), 3: 180-90; and H. Greeven, "προσκυνέω, προσκυνητής," in *Theological Dictionary of the New Testament*, 6: 764.

4. The pioneer work on the attitude of Jesus to the worship of his day is Ernst Lohmeyer's *Kultus und Evangelium,* first published in 1942. The English translation has the imaginative title *Lord of the Temple: A Study of the Relation between Cult and Gospel,* trans. Stewart Todd (Richmond: John Knox Press, 1962).

the inward devotion of the heart. "Beware of practicing your piety before men in order to be seen by them" (6:1). This does not mean that Jesus was opposed to public worship. Rather, he teaches us that because God is holy, our worship must be holy (5:48). God is in secret, God is transcendent, God is invisible, and therefore our worship must go beyond the merely visible and merely public. Outward piety must not be allowed to mask inward profanity. Worship is no place for whitened sepulchers.

The Gospel of John develops this theme in the dialogue between Jesus and the woman of Samaria — "But the hour is coming, and now is, when the true worshipers will worship the Father in spirit and truth, for such the Father seeks to worship him. God is spirit, and those who worship him must worship in spirit and truth" (4:23-24). In the Gospel of John, just as in the Gospel of Matthew, we learn that our worship must reflect the nature of God. God is spirit and therefore our worship must be in spirit and truth. By worship in spirit and truth Jesus meant worship that is an act of faith. The worshiper believes that God is faithful and merciful and therefore turns to him in time of need. The worship that is in spirit and truth is an act of love. It is not superstitious or compelled by fear; it is faithful to the truth. It does not try to fool, bribe, or force God but rather trusts God and the ways of God. True worship is not magical in the sense that it tries to control God but is rather obedient to God and according to God's Word. We worship God in spirit when our worship respects God's transcendence — that is, God's holiness, God's justice, God's truth. The worship that is in spirit and truth is spiritual in that it is inspired, directed, and filled with God's Spirit. As Raymond Brown has pointed out, it is the Holy Spirit who raises us above the earthly level and enables us to worship God truly.[5] True worship reflects what God is. It is holy

5. Brown, *The Gospel according to John I–XII,* Anchor Bible Series (Garden City, N.Y.: Doubleday, 1966), p. 180. See also R. Bultmann,

because God is holy (Matt. 5:48). It is spiritual because God is spirit (John 4:24). Both the Gospel of Matthew and the Gospel of John show Jesus as having taught what the prophets taught before him — namely, that our worship is to reflect God himself.

Another prominent expression of the prophetic doxology in the New Testament is found in the apostle Paul's words to the Romans, "I appeal to you therefore, brethren, by the mercies of God, to present your bodies as a living sacrifice, holy and acceptable to God, which is your spiritual worship" (12:1). For those who by the grace of God have entered into the new life in Christ, that life is the spiritual worship which reflects the glory of God and therefore worships God. This is the spiritual sacrifice of the royal priesthood mentioned in the second chapter of 1 Peter and the last chapter of Hebrews.[6] As Paul uses the term "spiritual worship," it refers to both the liturgical and the ethical dimensions of Christian experience. This worship has a long history behind it. The fact that the concept is encountered in so many levels of the tradition indicates that it had a broad currency in the early church. At least part of what was meant by "spiritual worship" was the worship that the Jews of the Exile had developed to replace the worship of the Jerusalem Temple. This they were forced to develop because the Law forbade much of the worship of the Temple from being offered anywhere other than in Jerusalem. This was particularly the case with the sacrifices. As a

---

"ἀλήθεια . . . ," in *Theological Dictionary of the New Testament*, 1: 246ff.; and E. Schweizer, "πνεῦμα, πνευματικός . . . ," in *Theological Dictionary of the New Testament*, 6: 437ff.

6. On the "spiritual worship" of the New Testament, see Otto Michel, *Der Brief an die Römer*, 4th ed. (Göttingen: Vandenhoeck & Ruprecht, 1966), pp. 290-94. See further the extended note of E. G. Selwyn, "The 'Spiritual House': Its Priesthood and Sacrifices," in *The First Epistle of St. Peter* (London: Macmillan, 1955), pp. 281-98. Selwyn attempts to bring together the various New Testament passages on spiritual worship.

replacement for this, the prophets had shown the Jews of the Exile an inner, more personal dimension of that worship which could be offered anywhere. The liturgical aspect of this "spiritual worship" consisted in the prayers, the psalms, and the study of Scripture.

The spiritual worship advocated by the New Testament does not mean spiritualized worship. A spiritualized worship that finds no place for such material things as money or bread and wine, or that objects to the use of art in worship because it is material rather than spiritual, is inspired by asceticism. Asceticism has often been confused with Christianity, but it springs from other sources. Yves Congar has given us a well-balanced study of the prophetic theology of worship in his *Le mystère du temple.* In this work he insists quite correctly that the spiritual nature of Christian worship does not compromise its concrete objective nature. Christian worship is at the same time both spiritual and corporal. The spiritual worship the apostle Paul would have us celebrate is the sacrifice of our bodies (Rom. 12:1). The spiritual songs he would have us sing are to be sung with our mouths (Col. 3:16; Eph. 5:19). Congar contends that it is important to see that the objective reality of the liturgy here on earth is more than simply the expression of a spiritual reality. It is the means of both its birth and its growth. Liturgical celebrations, Congar reminds us, are the means of realizing the spiritual worship.[7]

When Paul preached to the Athenians before the backdrop of the Acropolis, the citadel of the greatest artistic creations of ancient Greece, he told them, "Being then God's offspring, we ought not to think that the Deity is like gold, or silver, or stone, a representation by the art and imagination of man" (Acts 17:29). It is clear from this passage, just as it is clear from the Old Testament prophets, that gold, silver, and stone

---

7. Congar, *Le mystère du temple,* 2d ed. (Paris: Les Éditions du Cerf, 1963), pp. 220-26.

cannot reflect the nature of God; only human beings, God's offspring, can do that. The idols are misleading because they come from human imagination rather than divine revelation but even more importantly because God is revealed to the world not by art but by righteousness. I will have more to say about this shortly, but here let us simply note that this crucial text is telling us that art is not a form of revelation. Luke understands as well as the other New Testament writers the prophetic theology of worship. He presents Paul as making the same criticism of idolatry that the prophets had made before him.

Because the first Christians were so loyal to the prophetic heritage, their worship remained very simple for the first three centuries of their history. It was not until well into the Constantinian period that this began to change. One of the most interesting illustrations of the prophetic theology of worship in the literature of the ancient church is found in the work of Lactantius. Having become a Christian during the reign of Diocletian and having experienced the persecution of the pagan empire, he looks at Christian worship from the standpoint of the pre-Constantinian church. When Constantine did come into power, the first Christian emperor honored Lactantius by making him tutor to the imperial household, but by this time Lactantius was an old man. His understanding of Christian worship had been shaped in the old days before Christian worship had picked up the trappings of the imperial cult. His work is of interest to us because Lactantius, like Tertullian, came to his Christian faith out of Stoicism rather than neo-Platonism, and consequently he was open to aspects of Christian teaching that other early Christian thinkers neglected.

Lactantius was critical of the elaborate ceremonial of the pagan sacrifices. Like Tertullian before him, he contrasted the simplicity of Christian worship with the highly developed liturgy of Greek and Roman paganism. He insisted that it is innocence and purity of life that God wants from those who worship.[8] He ridiculed those who burned candles before statues of their gods. Did they believe their gods to dwell in darkness? For the Christian, Lactantius confesses, it makes more sense to devote all this attention to the poor, who are really images of God and yet unlike the idols have genuine needs.[9] When Lactantius tells us "the chief ceremonial in the worship of God is praise from the mouth of a just man,"[10] he is picking up the Stoic philosopher's criticism of the cultus of ancient Greece and Rome, but he is also picking up the prophets' criticism of the worship of the Temple.[11] The treatise "On True Worship," which Lactantius has left us in the sixth book of *The Divine Institutes,* has been ignored by liturgical scholars. This is most unfortunate, because Lactantius has preserved for us a significant theme of the doxology of the ante-Nicene church.

Of the greatest possible importance to the prophetic doxology is preaching. God is glorified when his Word is heard and obeyed. Without obedience to God's Word, there is no genuine service of worship. The Old Testament prophets were champions of the Law. They demanded that it be enforced when the politicians of the land would gladly have forgotten it. In the name of the Law of Moses, they championed the rights of the poor. The prophets were interpreters of the Law

8. See Lactantius, *The Divine Institutes,* 6.1-2, in *The Ante-Nicene Fathers,* 10 vols., ed. Alexander Roberts and James Donaldson et al. (New York: Christian Literature, 1885-1897), 7: 9-223. For the thoughts of Tertullian, see *On Baptism* 2, *On Idolatry* 13-16, and *Apology* 39, in *Ante-Nicene Fathers,* 3: 669, 68-71, and 46-47.

9. Lactantius, *Divine Institutes,* 6.13.

10. Lactantius, *Divine Institutes,* 6.25.

11. On the joining together of the prophetic and philosophic criticism of worship in antiquity, see Behm, *Theological Dictionary of the New Testament,* 3: 180-90. Clement of Alexandria is another early Christian writer who joins together both the philosophers' and the prophets' criticism of elaborate religious ceremonial. See Clement of Alexandria, *Stromata,* 8.5-8, in *The Ante-Nicene Fathers,* 2: 530-37.

who devoted themselves to making its meaning clear in very concrete historical situations. Many Christian preachers have maintained the prophetic tradition. One of the most obvious was John Chrysostom, who was distinguished not only as an interpreter of Holy Scripture but as a prophet as well. In his native Antioch, Chrysostom was known for his straight biblical preaching. He preached through one book of the Bible at a time, going verse by verse and chapter by chapter. His interpretations were straight in that they avoided the allegory Origen had encouraged and focused instead on the simple, straightforward meaning of the text. Today we call this approach the grammatical-historical interpretation.

Having won a solid reputation as both a biblical interpreter and a masterly orator, Chrysostom was called to Constantinople to become archbishop of the imperial city. He continued his expository preaching, but the more expository his preaching became, the more critical he was of the court. The extravagance, the pride in outward show, the unrestrained thirst for vainglory appeared to John Chrysostom as completely inconsistent with Christian faith. In preaching through Paul's Epistle to the Colossians, he felt constrained to preach against the luxury of the imperial household, where, it was rumored, silver chamber pots were in use. The whole of Constantinople was scandalized by the frankness of this criticism. But for John Chrysostom the issue was quite clear: the glory of God is compromised when mortals aspire to such vain pomp. The glory of God is totally other. It is justice, mercy, and holiness.

During the Middle Ages, God raised up a number of prophets who recalled the church in one way or another to purity of worship. The controversial Joachim of Fiore (ca. 1132-1202) preached the coming of an age of the Holy Spirit. His vision of the kingdom of God showed a deep understanding of the classic prophets of Israel. He had obviously studied Isaiah, Jeremiah, and Ezekiel with devotion. Joachim's preaching raised the vision of Christendom concerning the nature of Christian society. It must be admitted that the Joachite movement spawned a considerable amount of crass millenarianism, but the overall effect of the movement was to sharpen the demand for a more pious, more spiritual church life.

Jean Gerson (1363-1429) was another outstanding preacher who exercised a distinctly prophetic ministry. As chancellor of the University of Paris, he had access to the centers of leadership both in the kingdom of France and in the whole of Western Europe. It was particularly at the Council of Constance that Gerson brought his prophetic gifts to bear. For some years the Western church had been divided by the competing claims of rival popes. Finally an ecumenical council was called to meet in the city of Constance. The various contenders for the papal dignity were largely the pawns of secular rulers. Politics had subverted the spiritual concerns of the church. To a terribly secularized assembly of ecclesiastical politicians, Gerson preached conversion. As he saw it, nothing would heal the Great Schism so much as the spiritual rebirth of the religious leaders of the day.

Another important example of the prophetic ministry is Bernardino da Siena (1380-1444). Bernardino was the most notable of a whole series of Italian preachers who at the beginning of the Italian Renaissance exercised a remarkable prophetic ministry. Bernardino preached against gambling, women's cosmetics, elaborate fashions, unfair business practices, usury, pornographic art, and luxury of all sorts. His success in combating these evils was largely due to his sincerity and purity of character. While Bernardino was sympathetic to the learning of the Renaissance, he recognized that there was a good portion of paganism in it as well. Typically, that preeminently effective evangelist held his preaching campaigns during Lent in order that the people might be prepared to make their Easter communion. Even in Florence he was able to persuade his hearers to make clear their repentance by presenting their gaming tables, playing cards, and risqué books and paintings to be destroyed in a bonfire of vanities. Bernardino, as every true prophet, understood very well that one cannot serve both God and mammon. He recognized in the art and the culture, in the style and the luxury of Renaissance humanism, an incipient paganism that was essentially at variance with Christianity.

Fundamental to the reforms of early sixteenth-century Protestantism was the recovery of biblical Hebrew and the grammatical-historical interpretation of the Old Testament. In the upper Rhineland, Wolfgang Capito and John Oecolampadius led the way to a fresh reading of the Old Testament prophets.[12] Capito was the first Christian to attempt a Hebrew grammar. Then in 1528 he published a full commentary on the Hebrew text of the prophet Hosea. It was with his interpretation of the Hebrew text of Isaiah that Oecolampadius won the city of Basel to the Reformation. In time Oecolampadius did a whole series of commentaries on the Old Testament prophets. The commentary on Isaiah was followed by commentaries on Jeremiah and Ezekiel. These commentaries soon became a cooperative work. Oecolampadius lectured on the prophet, then Capito edited the material for publication as a commentary, and finally Konrad Pelikan developed an index. Eventually Pelikan published his own commentaries on the prophets. Before he died in 1531, Oecolampadius was able to complete the series with commentaries on the minor prophets and on Daniel. This intensive reexamination of the Old Testament prophets won great acclaim in the sixteenth century among Protestants and Catholics as well.

---

12. On the cooperation of Oecolampadius and Capito in the study of the Old Testament prophets, see E. Staehelin, *Das theologische Lebenswerk Oekolampads* (New York: Johnson Reprint, 1971), pp. 189-91, 396-409, 553-98. See also M. Kittelson, *Wolfgang Capito from Humanist to Reformer* (Leiden: E. J. Brill, 1975), especially pp. 208ff.

By the time Calvin wrote his commentaries on the prophets, he was able to draw on a wealth of new insight from the older Reformers. Calvin left us an important collection of commentaries on all of the prophetic books. He died while in the middle of his lectures on Ezekiel, but if he had been spared a few more months he would have produced complete commentaries on all the prophets. For us, however, the important thing to note is that this rethinking of the prophetic tradition by the Reformers of classical Protestantism was of the essence of their ministry. One of the things that became most clear to the Reformers was the prophetic doxology, and Calvin's commentaries on the Old Testament prophets are filled with appropriations of this strain of biblical doxology.[13]

The prophetic doxology, as we have already had occasion to remark, has been critical of what might be called the liturgical use of art — that is, the use of art in the service of worship as a means of focusing the devotion of the worshiper, not merely as decoration but as a means of grace, as, in some way, a parallel to Scripture or to the sacraments. The second commandment has been particularly difficult to observe in Western culture, where art has been so highly cultivated. There are all too many people, even in our modern culture, who have made art a substitute for religion. The Canaanites and the Philistines are still with us. Idolatry has proved itself a most persistent sin. And yet when the churches have filled up with paintings and sculpture and all kinds of *objets d'art,* the prophetic criticism has regularly revived. This has sometimes resulted in iconoclasm, as it did in the Byzantine Empire in the seventh century and as it did in the Peasants War at the

---

13. For passages in Calvin's commentaries that discuss the prophets' understanding of worship, see my article, "John Calvin and the Prophetic Criticism of Worship," in *John Calvin and the Church: A Prism of Reform,* ed. Timothy George (Louisville: Westminster/John Knox Press, 1990), pp. 230-46.

time of the Reformation. The classical Protestant Reformers — Luther, Zwingli, and Calvin — were opposed to iconoclasm. Regrettably, we have to be aware that art historians have often overlooked the distinction between the iconoclasts of the Peasants War and the Reformers of classical Protestantism. In the same way, liturgical historians seem to have overlooked the benefits of refusing the liturgical use of art. Sometimes the prophetic criticism of liturgical art has engendered some important artistic movements.[14]

One school of art that arose from a concern to observe the second commandment was Dutch seventeenth-century painting. The Reformation had taken very seriously the prophetic criticism of liturgical art, and yet the people of the Netherlands did love painting. Having accepted the Reformation, the Dutch church no longer commissioned artists to paint pictures of Christ and the apostles, the saints, and martyrs, which for centuries had been the primary subject matter of Christian painters. Altar pieces were not needed to tell the people of the heavenly mysteries celebrated by the priest in an unknown tongue. In the Protestant Netherlands the faithful were no longer illiterate. They had their Bibles, and they could read them. They did not need pictures to tell them what was in the sacred book. All this had its effect on the Christian painter, but there was something even more important. The whole neo-Platonic philosophy of art was obviated by the Protestant doctrine of

---

14. Cistercian architecture, for example, developed out of the conviction that luxury in church architecture constitutes a distraction from the devotional life. The Cistercian reform built solid monastic churches all through Europe during the Middle Ages. Among the most representative are Senanque, Le Thoronet, Noirlac, and Fontenay. Even today art historians have the highest regard for the aesthetic refinement of Cistercian architecture. On the Cistercian reform generally, see B. K. Lackner, *The Eleventh Century Background of Cîteaux* (Washington: Consortium Press, 1972); and L. J. Lekai, *The Cistercians, Ideals and Reality* (Kent, Ohio: Kent State University Press, 1977).

biblical revelation. No more was the painter an iconographer who understood it to be his vocation to reveal eternal mysteries.

The Dutch Protestant painters of the seventeenth century had to find a new way of understanding art. They did, of course, and what they came up with was very new in the history of religious art. Rembrandt became a biblical illustrator. His paintings and etchings of Abraham's sacrifice, David before King Saul, Esther's feast, Jesus preaching to the poor, and the supper at Emmaus all give us a very different approach to religious art. It is not iconographic; it is historical illustration. It is a sort of grammatical-historical depiction of the events of Scripture parallel to the grammatical-historical approach to biblical exegesis that the Reformers so admired. Those who write about art tend to deprecate illustration. This is unfortunate, for indeed it is an art, and Rembrandt was a master of it. Religious illustration is an art, but a different kind of art. One is not supposed to kneel down and pray before these pictures, nor is one supposed to hang them over an altar. Although they do engage our thoughts on their subjects, they are not supposed to stimulate meditation in the neo-Platonic sense. In these paintings there is no climbing of Jacob's ladder, no ascent into eternal realities. What we find is a powerful consciousness that the will of God can be lived in this particular historical time and geographical place. The biblical illustrations of Rembrandt are a sort of historical-grammatical illustration of Scripture that made Jesus the Savior of saints and sinners in seventeenth-century Holland. It is an art that makes no attempt to escape the realities of our time and place but rather to confront them. Rembrandt's Christ, apostles, disciples, and prophets and patriarchs of the Old Testament could be seen every day in Amsterdam. Rembrandt's biblical illustrations could be meditated upon, too, but the meditation would not lead one out of history into the timeless. It would lead one rather to the ultimate questions that meet us here and now. Pictures of Potiphar's wife and Bathsheba's bath make one realize what temptations plagued Rembrandt. Rembrandt's art tells us about his own religious struggles. It confronts the moral problems of his own life. Again and again the biblical illustrations raise the question of the love between father and son, a question so agonizing in Rembrandt's own life. Like Abraham, Rembrandt raised only one son. Three of his children died in infancy, and his sickly son Titus died as a very young man. Typology was very real for Rembrandt; he knew all about Abraham's sacrifice on Mount Moriah. He drew it again and again. Rembrandt's "Return of the Prodigal Son," painted in the last year of his life, is his final confession of faith. In the hands of Rembrandt, biblical illustration is art at its most profound.

Another aspect of the deeply religious art of the Netherlands is equally important even if it is less obvious. Rembrandt's art is objectively religious, but other Dutch artists produced a more subjective approach to religious art as well. They found ways of painting the scenes of common life in a religious light. There are those who see this art as purely secular and argue that the Dutch gave up religious art. But when one looks at Pieter de Hooch's interiors of well-ordered Dutch homes and sees a woman and her maid putting away the linens, a mother caring for her children, or an elderly man sitting in a light-filled room reading a book, one realizes something sacred is going on. There is something very beautiful about the calm and orderliness of the life de Hooch paints before us. He gives us a picture of what life can be. It can be beautiful!

One sees it even more clearly when one looks at Vermeer's allegory of fame. A woman is standing before a window with a most radiant light streaming in upon her. She is crowned with laurel and holding a trumpet and a book, the obvious symbols of the honor that in Vermeer's lifetime never came his way. Vermeer is always spoken of as the master of light, and indeed he was. The women he painted were always bathed in light — a woman in yellow standing before an open window reading a letter, a woman in blue holding a pitcher of water with light pouring onto her. One wonders what is intimated by the letter, the woman, the water, and the light. Vermeer seemed to love allegories, but he was much too respectful of the uniqueness of Scripture to treat Scripture itself allegorically. Unlike Origen, he understood the proper limits of allegory. Another obvious moral allegory is a painting of a woman weighing gold on a table beside a window. On the wall behind the woman is a faintly discernible picture of the Last Judgment. Again one perceives that in these paintings there is a weighing of values, a consideration of man's chief end. And yet these paintings of Vermeer are more than allegory. They are a seeking out of the beautiful. They show us that it is light which is ultimately beautiful. And the light that is beautiful is a very moral, very holy light.

Dutch seventeenth-century painting was not secularized at all. If it were, then why do we find all those vanitas paintings preaching the message of Ecclesiastes with a still life of tropical fruit, Chinese porcelains, exotic sea shells, and hybrid tulips? The vanitas paintings serve to set the limits of the enjoyment of beauty. The Dutch Calvinists were not ascetics. They loved the good things of creation. But they were ever mindful of the transcendent source of such blessings and ever aware of the duties of charity. This is all very clear when one looks at the whole of Dutch Protestant painting in all its breadth and variety. In fact, one of the amazing things about Dutch painting is the way it discovers beauty in things that others might consider mundane. Cattle, barnyards, mills, and fishing boats are all discovered to have a beauty. The essence of the Dutch masters is that they discovered beauty in the little things of life. Dutch landscapes are amazing! What beauty they find in that modest land! It is so colorless and so flat. It has none of the drama of the Italian landscape, and yet the Dutch painters discovered its beauties, the shimmer of its waters and the utter majesty of its light-filled skies. Dutch landscapes have an amazing way of concentrating on the heavens.

Dutch painting was deeply religious, but it made no pretense about being iconographical. It might meditate on Scripture, but it is not Scripture. The Dutch never even thought of confusing art and revelation. They never even toyed with the idea that an artist might be inspired in a way similar to the apostles and the prophets. No one even suggested that a biblical preacher and a biblical illustrator might be doing the same thing. Their view of the ministry of the Word was something very well defined. The Word of God was quite unique. Painting was a craft in a culture that valued fine craftsmanship. It was the craft of making things beautiful. One might even call it the craft of discovering beauty. It was, to be sure, a very intellectual craft, but it was a craft just the same. It was a human work through and through, but it was a human work in a society that valued human work. Painters belonged to a guild, like weavers, cabinet makers, and silversmiths, and there was a genuine nobility in belonging to a guild in the Dutch merchant republic. Work was a sacred responsibility. Six days they labored and did all their work, but the Sabbath was a day of rest. God had commanded the weekday work just as he had commanded the worship of the Lord's Day. One needed to work and one needed to worship, but good Dutch Protestants never confused the two. Art and worship are things quite different.

One of Scotland's great prophets was Thomas Guthrie (1803-1875). Pastor of the Church of the Grayfriars in Edinburgh, Guthrie was given an amazingly clear insight into the miseries that the Industrial Revolution had brought to the population of the city. He was the Charles Dickens of the Scottish pulpit. Unlike many prophets, he was able to win the support of many of the leading citizens of the day. He was the son of a devout banking family, and yet he was zealous in his concern to improve the lot of the poor. His culture, his compassion, his warm, virile piety all succeeded in securing an acceptance of his sermons among the leading legislators, bankers, and industrialists of the city. One of his best-known series of sermons, *The City: Its Sins, Its Sorrows,* is an exposition of the text of Luke 19:41, "he beheld the city, and wept over it" (KJV). He takes the well-known text that tells of Jesus weeping over Jerusalem and applies it to Edinburgh. In vivid detail he paints the miseries of the city, its tenement houses, its saloons, and its sweatshops. The sermons sensitized the conscience of that very Christian city. Far from inciting a sort of Marxist class warfare, Guthrie appealed to the Christian leadership of the city to enact child labor laws, to provide education for the children of the poor, to curb the liquor traffic, and to give humane care to fallen women and illegitimate children. With the backing Guthrie got not only from his congregation but from the city as a whole, many of the reforms he proposed actually came into existence.

A positive contribution of twentieth-century American Protestantism to the theology of worship has been its development of the concept of stewardship. The giving of alms for the support of the suffering, the poor, and the neglected has become an increasingly important liturgical concern. This is expressed by the fact that the collection of alms is made during the service of worship rather than before it or after it. This was not the older practice; there has always been a certain hesitancy about collecting alms during worship. Some have tried to fit the giving of alms into worship by thinking of it as an offering rather than as a collection and have even gone so far as to raise it up to heaven in a gesture of presenting it to God and then laying it on some kind of altar. But there is no need to justify the collection of alms by such ceremonial. The apostle Paul clearly admonished his followers to collect contributions for charitable purposes on the Lord's Day. A highly ceremonial offertory is theologically misleading at best. Much to be preferred is a straightforward collection of alms for the poor together with tithes for the support of the church. No further ceremony is needed. When this collection is made at the end of the service of worship, the connection between the service of God and the service of the neighbor becomes very clear. Faithful Christian worship issues in generous Christian service.

# VI

## Covenantal Doxology

Finally, let us direct our attention to *covenantal doxology*. Covenantal doxology emphasizes that when the assembly of God's people is united in sacred bond, giving thanks for the works of redemption, confessing their covenantal obligations, and witnessing to the faithfulness of God, then God is worshiped.

Most helpful for understanding the roots of Christian doxology is the covenantal meal recorded in the twenty-fourth chapter of Exodus.[1] There Moses reads to the assembled people the book of the covenant, and the people make a vow: "All that the LORD has spoken we will do, and we will be obedient" (v. 7). Then Moses takes the blood of the sacrifice, sprinkles half of it on the altar and half on the people. This signifies the covenantal union that brought God and his people together in a common life. "Behold the blood

1. For a brief discussion of this passage and its relation to the covenant theology of the Old Testament, see Brevard S. Childs, *The Book of Exodus* (Philadelphia: Westminster Press, 1974), pp. 497-511. For more detailed discussion, see L. Perlitt, *Bundestheologie im Altentestament* (Neukirchen-Vluyn: Verlag des Erziehungsvereins, [1969]); Rolf Rendtorff, *Studien zur Geschichte des Opfers im Alten Israel* (Neukirchen-Vluyn: Verlag des Erziehungsvereins, 1967); and R. Schmid, *Das Bundesopfer in Israel* (Munich: Köselverlag, 1964).

of the covenant which the LORD has made with you in accordance with all these words" (v. 8). Surely these words make very clear the relation of the proclamation of the Word to our communion with God: to enter into the presence of God goes together with entering into a new order of life. Finally, Moses took the elders up on the mountain, and "they beheld God, and ate and drank" (v. 11). The meaning of this is just as clear: in the sharing of the meal one enters into table fellowship with God. From the standpoint of biblical imagery, this is fellowship or, even better, communion at its most intimate. It means to enter into God's household, or family. The imagery conveys the profound nature of the covenantal bond. But there is something more. This passage is interesting because it suggests to the Christian theologian a way of understanding the relation of Word and sacrament in worship. As we have seen, the covenantal bond is made on the basis of "all these words." This suggests that the sprinkling and the eating, which Christians have usually seen as a type of baptism and the Lord's Supper, seal the covenant which is proclaimed in the reading of the book of the covenant and confessed by the vow of faith. The implication of all this for the understanding of our own worship is rich indeed!

Although thanksgiving is not mentioned in this passage, the thankful memorial of God's redemptive acts is central to the covenantal doxology. There are plenty of other passages of Scripture, as we shall see, where this becomes clear. It was because in time of need one had called on God for help and he had heard that cry that one was, ever after, obligated to recite God's saving acts as thanksgiving. This thanksgiving confessed to God the obligation one now owed to him as redeemer and witnessed to the assembly of the faithful God's saving power.

The various aspects of covenantal thanksgiving are found in the Hebrew word *yadah*, which means not only "thanksgiv-

112

ing" but "confession" and "witness" as well.[2] Thanksgiving is a religious service that is owed to God by those whom God has saved in their time of need. It is a recognition or confession of our obligation to our redeemer. Beyond that, it is a witness both to the faithful and to the world of God's saving power. As such it encourages and builds up the neighbor as one witness confirms another. Finally, thanksgiving is worship because the multitude of the witnesses magnifies God's glory. To be sure, thanksgiving is often used as a synonym for praise in Scripture, but as similar as they may be in general, praise and thanksgiving each have a particular place in the doxology of Scripture.[3] From the standpoint of covenantal theology, thanksgiving recites the mighty acts of God for our salvation.

These eucharistic recitals could take place at different points in the worship of Israel.[4] We read for instance in Deuteronomy 26:5-9 that at the offering of the firstfruits, one is to appear at the sanctuary with one's offering and confess, "A wandering Aramean was my father; and he went down into Egypt and sojourned there, few in number; and there he became a nation, great, mighty, and populous. And the Egyptians treated us harshly, and afflicted us, and laid upon us hard bondage. Then we cried to the LORD the God of our fathers, and the LORD heard our voice, and saw our affliction, our toil, and our oppression; and the LORD brought us out of Egypt with a mighty hand and an outstretched arm, with great terror, with signs and wonders; and he brought us into this place and

2. Sigmund Mowinckel's discussion of thanksgiving psalms is still helpful for an understanding of covenantal thanksgiving; see *The Psalms in Israel's Worship*, 2 vols. (Nashville: Abingdon Press, 1962), 2: 26-43.

3. On the distinction between praise and thanksgiving, see my article "The Psalms of Praise in the Worship of the New Testament Church," *Interpretation* 39 (1985): 20-33.

4. On the recital of holy history in the worship of ancient Israel, see G. von Rad, *Old Testament Theology*, 2 vols., trans. D. M. G. Stalker (Edinburgh: Oliver & Boyd, 1962), 1: 121-35.

gave us this land, a land flowing with milk and honey." At the feast of Passover, thanksgiving for God's mighty acts of redemption has a significant place. In the Passover Haggadah, the father is to recount to the son the story of God's deliverance of Israel from Egypt. Then again at the close of the meal, thanksgiving is to be made for the mighty acts of redemption over the cup of blessing. This prayer never had an official formulation, but there were definite traditions about its formulation. It would have gone something like this:

> Blessed you are, O LORD, our God,
> > King of the universe,
> for you have fed the whole world
> > with your goodness.
> In grace, love, and mercy,
> > you have given bread to all flesh
> > for your lovingkindness is everlasting.
> According to your everlasting goodness
> > you have not left us in want,
> > neither will you leave us in need
> > in eternity, for your name's sake.
> For you feed and care for all
> > and provide for all your creation.
> Blessed you are, O LORD,
> > for you provide for all.

> We give thanks to you, O LORD, our God,
> For you have given to our fathers
> > the good and wide land of Israel.
> For you, O LORD, our God, have led them out of
> > the land of Egypt
> > and ransomed them from the house of bondage.
> We give thanks to you for your covenant
> > which you have sealed to us in the rite of circumcision.
> For your Law
> > which you have taught us,

114

For the commandments
    which you have revealed,
For life, care, and love
    with which you have blessed us. . . .
Blessed you are, O Lord,
    for you have given us this land and filled it with food.[5]

In later generations these two benedictions were expanded with a thanksgiving for the election of Jerusalem and the covenant with the house of David, but basically it was a prayer of thanksgiving for God's mighty acts of creation and redemption. As time went on, this thanksgiving over the cup of blessing assumed great importance in the Christian liturgy. It seems to have been this prayer that evolved into what today Christian liturgical scholars call "The Eucharistic Prayer," the long prayer of thanksgiving that is said over the bread and wine at the communion service.

The book of Psalms has preserved a number of covenantal thanksgivings.[6] From the standpoint of the theology of worship, Psalm 105 is perhaps the most clearly focused of these. The psalm begins with a dazzling constellation of liturgical ideas.

O give thanks to the Lord, call on his name,
    make known his deeds among the peoples!

---

5. H. L. Strack and P. Billerbeck, *Kommentar zum neuen Testament aus Talmud und Midrasch,* 6 vols. (Munich: C. H. Beck, 1922-1961), IV/2: 631.

6. One does not have to follow Arthur Weiser to the extent of explaining all the psalms in terms of a festival of covenant renewal in order to recognize in the historical psalms the importance of thanksgiving to covenantal doxology. See Weiser, *The Psalms: A Commentary* (Philadelphia: Westminster Press, 1962), pp. 23-52. For a significant criticism of Weiser's position, see Hans-Joachim Kraus, *Theologie der Psalmen,* Biblischer Kommentar altes Testaments nr. 15, Band 3 (Neukirchen-Vluyn: Neukirchener Verlag, 1979), pp. 64-71. Still helpful are the insights on the thanksgiving psalms of Mowinckel, *The Psalms in Israel's Worship,* 2: 26-43.

Sing to him, sing praises to him,
　　tell of all his wonderful works!
Glory in his holy name;
　　let the hearts of those who seek the LORD rejoice!
Seek the LORD and his strength,
　　seek his presence continually!
Remember the wonderful works that he has done,
　　his miracles, and the judgments he uttered,
O offspring of Abraham his servant,
　　sons of Jacob, his chosen ones!

He is the LORD our God;
　　his judgments are in all the earth.
He is mindful of his covenant for ever,
　　of the word that he commanded, for a thousand
　　　　generations,
the covenant which he made with Abraham,
　　his sworn promise to Isaac. (Vv. 1-9)

To give thanks is to make known the mighty acts of redemption by which God laid claim to Israel. This is both thanksgiving to God and a witness to the peoples. The acts of redemption are made known in hymnic song, and in this sacred remembrance the presence of God is experienced. Those who have sought God rejoice at having found the one they sought. This thanksgiving is the grateful memorial made by the covenant people of the benefits of the covenant. Through this memorial, the covenant is renewed generation after generation, and by giving thanks for the holy history, one claims one's place in that history. Having made all this quite clear, the psalm recounts at length the sacred history from the covenant made with Abraham to Israel's entrance into the Promised Land. The thankful recounting of how God saved us when we were lost is the ever-recurring witness of his people.

That the New Testament had a covenantal understanding of worship is clear from the First Epistle to the Corinthians where the apostle Paul instructs his followers on a number of matters having to do with worship.[7] Christians cannot participate in pagan cultic meals, for "The cup of blessing which we bless, is it not a participation in the blood of Christ? The bread which we break, is it not a participation in the body of Christ?" (1 Cor. 10:16). The thanksgiving over the cup of blessing is obviously of considerable importance in the celebration of the Lord's Supper.[8] Because Christians have shared the Lord's Supper, a covenantal bond has been established between them and Christ. This covenantal bond is exclusive and obligates them to Christ alone. "You cannot partake of the table of the Lord and the table of demons" (10:21). Then a bit further on in the following chapter, the apostle turns to another aspect of Christian worship. At this point he focuses even more specifically on the nature of the celebration of the Lord's Supper, speaking of "when you assemble as a church" (11:18). This phrase has tremendous implications for our understanding of worship. It implies that the assembling together is of the essence of worship. This would, of course, make infinite sense from the standpoint of a covenantal doxology. Joining together in sacred fellowship with God and with each other is worship. In fact, that is what the church is: an assembly that has been called out for the service of God. That is what the word *church* means: an assembly of those who have been called out.

7. It is Eduard Schweizer who has most effectively called our attention back to the importance of the covenant aspect of the New Testament understanding of the Lord's Supper. See Schweizer, *The Lord's Supper according to the New Testament,* trans. James M. Davis (Philadelphia: Fortress Press, 1967).

8. On the prayer of thanksgiving over the cup of blessing, see J. P. Audet, "Esquisse historique du genre litteraire de la bènèdiction juife et de l'eucharistie chrétienne," *Revue Biblique* 65 (1958): 371-99; and Joachim Jeremias, *The Eucharistic Words of Jesus,* trans. Norman Perrin (Philadelphia: Fortress Press, 1977).

Now Paul turns to a particular problem in the celebration of the Lord's Supper. The Supper had become a feast in which those who had plenty feasted while the poorer members of the community went hungry. In the covenant bond, those who have plenty must share with those who do not. It is indeed a covenant meal! With an obvious reference to Exodus 24:8, the apostle reminds them of the words of Jesus, "This cup is the new covenant in my blood" (1 Cor. 11:25). This makes it even clearer that the Lord's Supper is to be understood in covenantal terms. Then in chapters 12 to 14, Paul addresses certain questions about prayer and preaching in public worship. There were those who claimed certain spiritual gifts that tended to break the bond of love. Although speaking in tongues may be a part of worship, it must not be allowed to become a matter of pride or to weaken the bond of love. In chapter 13 we find the apostle's famous teaching on love. In chapter 14 he tells the Corinthians that when they come together for worship, they are to have hymns, reading from Scripture, and preaching.[9] Perhaps they might have speaking in tongues if there is an interpretation, but whatever is done should be done for building up the body of Christ (14:26). It is the covenantal bond of love that worship is to promote, whether in the Supper, in prayer, or in preaching.

I should point out here that the reason this passage of 1 Corinthians had to be written was that the covenantal meal had been debased into what it has sadly become among all too many Americans — a fellowship supper and nothing more. What makes a covenant meal more than simply one more convivial gathering is the moral resolve that "All that

9. On the worship of the early church, see Gerhard Delling, *Worship in the New Testament* (Philadelphia: Westminster Press, 1962); C. F. D. Moule, *Worship in the New Testament* (Richmond: John Knox Press, 1967); and Willy Rordorf, *La liturgie, foi, et vie des premiers chrétiens* (Paris: Beauchesne, 1986), pp. 317-42.

the LORD has spoken we will do" (Exod. 24:7). A covenantal meal is an occasion of high seriousness. The apostle Paul made it very clear when he reminded the Corinthians that it was the same night on which Jesus had been betrayed that he instituted this meal. It is not to be entered into casually. Down through the centuries the church has been fairly consistent in insisting on a definite discipline of admission to the Lord's Table. When this discipline is ignored, the covenant meal rather quickly degenerates into a fellowship supper, and the old problem of the Corinthians is upon us again.

The covenantal theology of worship appears quite clearly during the patristic period. The North African theologians had a particularly strong sense of the covenantal dimension of their worship. When Tertullian calls baptism a *sacramentum* — that is, a vow or a pledge of allegiance — the very choice of that word implies a covenantal understanding of worship.[10] The Latin word *sacramentum* was used to denote the vow of faithfulness or pledge of allegiance that a soldier made to his commander on entering military service. It served as a sign given to indicate that one was part of a specific community or group. In the first instance it was the reciting of the Apostles' Creed that Tertullian called a *sacramentum*. This was obviously appropriate because the Creed was the vow of faith that was made at the time of baptism. The vow of faith was of great moment in Tertullian's understanding of things. It was of the essence of baptism, and so quite naturally it led Tertullian to speak of baptism as a *sacramentum* as well.

Augustine, another North African, emphasizes the covenantal aspect of worship in his *De doctrina christiana*. The

10. On the etymology of the word *sacramentum,* see Christine Mohrmann, "Sacramentum dans les plus anciens texts chrétiens," *Etudes sur le latin des Chrétiens,* 3 vols. (Rome, 1958-1965), 1: 233-44; and Hans von Soden, "Μυστήριον und *sacramentum* in den ersten zwei Jahrhunderten der Kirche," *Zeitschrift für die neutestamentliche Wissenschaft* 12 (1911): 211-12.

whole point of Christian preaching is to strengthen the bond of love that unites the Christian community to God. Those who truly understand the Scriptures, according to Augustine, interpret them in such a way that they tend to build up a twofold love — first, love for God, and second, love for the neighbor.[11] Augustine's theology of worship, as is obvious from the whole of this work, leans very heavily on the thirteenth chapter of 1 Corinthians. It is love that is the purpose of coming together as a Christian fellowship to worship God. Augustine well understood those chapters of 1 Corinthians that we have just considered. It is on this passage that he built his theology of worship. The spiritual gifts of prophecy, of preaching, and of teaching, the gift of tongues, the utterance of prayer, and the celebration of the Supper all have their purpose in strengthening the bond of love. For Augustine as for the apostle Paul, worship is an expression of covenant fellowship both with God and with the Christian community.

At the time of the Protestant Reformation, it was Luther who first proposed that it might be from covenant theology that one could best explain the sacraments. Luther and the other Reformers found the traditional Scholastic approach to sacramental theology quite inadequate for explaining much in Christian worship. In *The Babylonian Captivity of the Church* he suggests a covenantal theology of the sacraments as an alternative to Scholastic theology.[12] Luther tells us of how God made covenantal promises to Noah, Abraham, and Gideon and then confirmed these promises with signs of the covenant. In another less well-known work of Luther's, *A Treatise on the New Testament, That Is the Holy Mass,* written

11. Augustine, *On Christian Doctrine,* in *Nicene and Post-Nicene Fathers,* series 1, 14 vols., ed. Philip Schaff (New York: Christian Literature, 1886-1890), 2: 533ff.

12. See especially Luther, *The Babylonian Captivity of the Church,* in *Luther's Works,* 55 vols., ed. Jaroslav Pelikan and Helmut T. Lehmann (Philadelphia: Fortress Press, 1955-), 36: 37-57.

in the same year, we discover the Reformer delving more deeply into a covenantal theology of the sacraments. He contends that the central thing in the Lord's Supper is the promise found in the words of institution, "This is my body broken for you. . . . This is my blood poured out for many for the remission of sins." It is through promises that God works with us, says Luther. God gives us a promise that we might receive it by faith. We find such promises all through both the Old Testament and the New. God made promises to Adam, to Noah, to Abraham, and to Moses. "In the New Testament, likewise, Christ made a promise or solemn vow, which we are to believe and thereby come to righteousness and salvation. This promise is the words . . . 'This is the cup of the New Testament.' "[13] In explaining what Jesus meant, Luther goes on to say, "In all his promises, moreover, in addition to the word, God has usually given a sign, for the greater assurance and strengthening of our faith."[14] God gave the rainbow to Noah and circumcision to Abraham as signs and seals of the covenant. Luther's proposal for a new approach to understanding the sacraments is, quite simply, that we understand them as signs of the covenant. To do this is to understand the sacraments by means of concepts that are thoroughly biblical rather than Scholastic.

And yet it was not Luther who followed up his suggestion but rather the Swiss Reformer Henry Bullinger.[15] Originally Bullinger developed his covenant theology as a means of understanding the function of infant baptism. He soon found

13. Luther, *A Treatise on the New Testament, That Is the Holy Mass,* in *Luther's Works,* 35: 84.

14. Luther, *A Treatise on the New Testament,* p. 86.

15. For a more detailed presentation of Bullinger's covenantal understanding of the sacraments, see *The Decades of Henry Bullinger,* 5 vols., ed. Thomas Harding (Cambridge: Cambridge University Press, 1849-1852), 4: 226-92. See also Joachim Staedtke, *Die theologie des jungen Bullinger* (Zurich: Zwingli Verlag, 1962), pp. 227-54.

it just as helpful in explaining the Lord's Supper. What Luther had outlined with a rapid pen Bullinger filled in with all the color of thorough biblical research. He delved even more thoroughly into the biblical concept of covenant as well as the concepts of sign, memorial, and thanksgiving. The elaborate covenant theology that Bullinger developed has had an abiding influence in Protestant circles. In Calvin's *Institutes of the Christian Religion* we find that Reformer developing a covenantal understanding of the Lord's Supper as well. He, too, explains the Supper as the sealing of the covenant promises proclaimed in the Word.[16]

In eighteenth-century Scotland, a land where classical Protestantism was cultivated with the utmost seriousness, covenantal theology was basic to the understanding of worship. This was particularly obvious in the celebration of the Lord's Supper. By the year 1700, the Scottish communion season had become a well-established liturgical institution. Several times a year communion was celebrated in each church, and the better part of a week was given to this celebration. People from neighboring congregations would join in, and guest preachers would be invited to take part. During the middle of the week a series of preparatory services was held. At these services sermons would be preached encouraging the faithful to examine their lives to see if they had been faithful to their covenant vows. Celebration and discipline were kept in careful balance. No one ever mistook a Scottish communion service for a coffee klatch. The need of repentance and the assurance of salvation were clearly set forth. Psalms of lamentation and confession were sung, and the minister led the congregation in appropriate prayers. These prayers were presented as examples of the sorts of prayers that each member of the congregation should be offering in the secret confines of his or her own prayer closet. "Secret" or "closet" prayer,

16. See Calvin, *Institutes of the Christian Religion,* 4.14.6.

as devout Protestants of that period called it, was an integral part of the total religious life.

John Willison (1680-1750), minister of the Scottish city of Dundee, gives us about as faithful a picture of classic Scottish worship as we could find.[17] His preparatory sermons make very clear the importance of preparing for the sacrament in secret prayer. The covenant vows of faith were to be made in secret prayer and confirmed publicly by participation in the sacrament. Secret prayer was a preparation for public prayer, just as public prayer had been the pattern for secret prayer. The congregation came well prepared to make their solemn vows in public and to enter into the prayers of the service. The prayers were in a special way vows, and they could not be entered into lightly. They were sacred promises to follow Christ more closely and to love him more deeply. They required deliberation and forethought. All this was made quite explicit in John Willison's preparatory sermons. When the congregation came to the Lord's Supper, the covenant vows were to be sealed by sharing in the loaf and the cup of the covenant meal. A hymn that would have been sung very often at these preparatory services was the paraphrase of Jacob's prayer at Bethel:

O God of Bethel, by whose hand
Thy people still are fed;
Who through this weary pilgrimage
Hast all our fathers led,

17. The most important of Willison's works are his *Treatise concerning the Sanctification of the Lord's Day* (1712), *A Sacramental Directory* (1716), *Five Sacramental Sermons* (1722), and *Sacramental Meditations* (1747). These works were frequently reprinted in Great Britain and America throughout the eighteenth century and well into the middle of the nineteenth century. This alone demonstrates how important they were in nourishing popular piety. A convenient collection of these and other of Willison's works on worship is *The Practical Works,* ed. W. M. Hetherington (London: Blackie & Son, [ca. 1830]).

Our vows, our prayers, we now present
Before Thy throne of grace;
God of our fathers, be the God
Of their succeeding race.

Through each perplexing path of life
Our wandering footsteps guide;
Give us each day our daily bread,
And raiment fit provide.

O spread Thy covering wings around
Till all our wanderings cease,
And at our Father's loved abode
Our souls arrive in peace.

Such blessings from Thy gracious hand
Our humble prayers implore;
And Thou shalt be our chosen God
And portion evermore.

These "Scottish Paraphrases" were the canticles of the Church of Scotland, and this particular hymn was a favorite for the celebration of both communion and baptism. Nothing could have made the covenantal nature of Scottish worship more explicit.

For most of the members of the congregation these communion seasons were a time for renewing their covenant vows, but there were always those, particularly among the young people, for whom this would be the first communion. It was expected that before young people were admitted to the table they would have memorized the Westminster Shorter Catechism. In the week before the communion they would recite the catechism to the minister and the elders. Being admitted to the Lord's Table by the elders was what constituted joining the church. This was not understood as confirmation but as admission to the Lord's Supper. One could assume that the young people had been baptized in infancy. The reciting of the catechism was a profession of faith, the faith into which they had been baptized. It was the making of the covenant vows, and the sealing of those vows with the covenant meal, that made one a member of the church.

Having made these very thorough preparations for the Lord's Supper, when the Lord's Day morning finally arrived, the people would celebrate the sacrament. This was the time when the gospel was proclaimed in its simplest, most essential, and most direct manner. No minister would have dreamed of coming up with some little communion meditation, short enough so that the service would not become too long. If he had made any false moves in that direction, the congregation would have been scandalized. It was at the communion service that one expected to hear evangelistic preaching at its fullest and most complete. This is evident in the communion sermons of one Scottish preacher after another. As late as the beginning of the nineteenth century, Andrew Thomson, minister of St. George's Church in Edinburgh, gives us a typical Scottish communion sermon preaching on the text, "God commendeth his love toward us, in that, while we were yet sinners, Christ died for us" (Rom. 5:8, KJV).[18] This for Thomson was the heart of the gospel, and that was what was to be preached at the sacrament, because it was there that the gospel was accepted by faith.

When the sermon was finished, the congregation would gather about the table. This was an important symbolic act. The minister and the elders would take their place behind the table while the members would sit around the remaining three sides. With the bread and wine set before him, the minister would offer a long and comprehensive prayer of thanksgiving for God's mighty acts of creation and redemption. The min-

18. Thomson, *Sermons and Sacramental Exhortations* (London, 1831), pp. 32ff. See also Willison, *The Practical Works,* pp. 303ff. and 557ff.

ister would no doubt follow the example of the prayer of John Knox in the *Book of Common Order,* but he would have prepared himself to lead this prayer, filling it with expressions of praise and thanksgiving as well as the recounting of the history of salvation. The prayer finished, the elders would serve table, with the people passing both the bread and the cup one to another. That all participated in serving and being served was seen as part of the sacred sign.

On Sunday evening there was normally a thanksgiving service, followed by another thanksgiving service on Monday. Here the implications of the covenant relationship were stressed. One preached on the benefits of the covenant and the covenant duties. There were more psalms and more prayers, and there was probably a collection of alms for the relief of the needy. The psalms sung at these thanksgiving services were quite naturally the votive thanksgiving psalms with their strong covenantal themes, which give particular expression to the fact that receiving the grace of God lays upon us the obligation to consecrate our lives to his service.

> I love the Lord, because my voice
>   and prayers he did hear.
> I, while I live, will call on him,
>   who bow'd to me his ear.
>
> I'll of salvation take the cup,
>   on God's name will I call:
> I'll pay my vows now to the Lord
>   before his people all.
> Dear in God's sight is his saints' death.
>   Thy servant, Lord, am I;
> Thy servant sure, thine handmaid's son:
>   my bands thou didst untie.
>
> Thank-off'rings I to thee will give,
>   and on God's name will call.

126

I'll pay my vows now to the Lord
   before his people all;
Within the courts of God's own house,
   within the midst of thee,
O city of Jerusalem.
   Praise to the Lord give ye.[19]

With the coming of the Great Awakening, the covenantal aspect of the celebration of the Lord's Supper was strengthened in a new direction. The ministry of Jacobus Theodorus Frelinghuysen to the Dutch Reformed congregations of New Jersey's Raritan Valley is usually regarded as one of the sources of this movement. Another source would, of course, have been the ministry of Jonathan Edwards in the Connecticut Valley. The Great Awakening was one of the definitive experiences of American Christianity. It was one of those experiences that makes us what we are as a Christian people. It forged a bond among the churches of all thirteen colonies. If one may use a figure of speech, it was a spiritual baptism that made them all one body. Having been influenced by Continental pietism, Frelinghuysen put a strong emphasis on the conversion experience.[20] Beginning in New Brunswick and going up and down the Raritan River and its tributaries, he preached and catechized in the Dutch-speaking communities of central New Jersey. His labors produced a group of churches characterized by devotional fervor and moral seriousness. Frelinghuysen's ministry had a great influence on young Gilbert Tennent, pastor of the English-speaking church at New Brunswick. He began to preach for conversion just as Frelinghuysen had. Tennent's sermons

19. Psalm 116:1-2, 13-19, in *The Scottish Psalter, 1929,* ed. Geoffrey Cumberlege (London: Oxford University Press, 1929), pp. 148-49.
20. See James Tanis, *Dutch Calvinistic Pietism in the Middle Colonies: A Study of the Life and Theology of Theodorus Jacobus Frelinghuysen* (The Hague: Martinus Nijhoff, 1967).

caught fire, and before long the two preachers, one preaching in Dutch and the other in English, had a full-scale revival going.

Tennent's evangelistic preaching attracted considerable attention throughout the English-speaking colonies, and a collection of his sermons was published in New York in 1735, and again in Boston in 1739.[21] It is particularly interesting that these evangelistic sermons were sacramental sermons — that is, sermons preached at a celebration of the sacrament of the Lord's Supper. For the preachers of the Great Awakening, evangelism clearly had a sacramental dimension. It was at the celebration of communion that those who had heard the preaching of the gospel and had believed it made their vows of faith by participation in the sacrament. The reciting of the Apostles' Creed in the course of the celebration made this explicit, but the sharing of the meal itself was understood as the sealing of the covenant. Ever since the covenant was given to Abraham, there had been an evangelistic aspect to it. The covenant promised to bless Abraham with descendants as numerous as the stars of the sky and the sands of the seashore. To the descendants of Abraham it promised the land as their heritage and then promised that in God's blessing of his covenant people all the nations of the earth would be blessed. This opening up of the covenant to all peoples has been at the heart of American Christianity ever since. Covenant implies evangelism.

At about the same time the Great Awakening was bringing revival to the churches of America, the Wesleys were experiencing an equally intense renewal of the Christian faith in England. Charles Wesley developed a covenantal understanding of worship in his hymnody.

21. The New York edition bears the title *The Espousals; or, A Passionate Perswasive to a Marriage with the Lamb of God* (New York: J. Peter Zenger, 1735).

Come, let us use the grace divine,
    And all with one accord,
In a perpetual covenant join
    Ourselves to Christ the Lord.

Give up ourselves, through Jesu's power,
    His name to glorify;
And promise in this sacred hour
    For God to live and die.

The covenant we this moment make
    Be ever kept in mind!
We will no more our God forsake,
    Or cast his words behind.

We never will throw off his fear
    Who hears our solemn vow;
And if thou art well pleased to hear,
    Come down, and meet us now!

Thee, Father, Son, and Holy Ghost,
    Let all our hearts receive!
Present with the celestial host,
    The peaceful answer give!

To each the covenant-blood apply
    Which takes our sins away;
And register our names on high,
    And keep us to that day![22]

We gather from this that for Charles Wesley the coming together of the Christian congregation for worship is an affirmation of the covenant, a promise to live one's life in the service of God. In fact, the very singing of the hymn is a creedal statement, a

22. Wesley, *Short Hymns on Select Passages of the Holy Scriptures*, 2 vols. (Bristol: Farley, 1762), 2: 36ff.

confession of faith, and a covenant vow. One might say that Wesley's theology of hymnody is covenantal. In worship God graciously applies to believers the blood of the covenant which empowers them to keep the covenant promises.

Karl Barth attempted to get back behind the Protestant theology of the seventeenth and eighteenth centuries and rediscover the classical Protestantism of the Reformation period. He was hardly an admirer of either Protestant orthodoxy or pietism, but even at that he developed a distinctly covenantal theology of worship. Like Augustine and Calvin before him, Barth unfolded his theology of worship in his interpretation of Christ's summary of the Law, that we are to love God with our whole being and our neighbors as ourselves.[23] As Barth sees it, true worship takes place in the covenantal bond of love. "Christian love cannot be understood except as thankfulness which the believer owes to God."[24] To love God is to be thankful to God and to witness to the neighbor of God's graciousness. This thankfulness and this witness take place in the context of the concrete celebration of baptism and the Lord's Supper. It can be done only because "In holy baptism I am placed by the Church under the promise of the Holy Ghost."[25] It can be done only because "In the Lord's Supper I am nourished by the Church on the true body and blood of Christ to eternal life."[26] This thanksgiving and this witness is the purpose of the Christian life. As Barth puts it, "The fulness of His love is not only that He rescues us from . . . sin and death, . . . but that He claims us for the proclamation of His glory."[27] To worship is to love God, but it is also to love the

23. See Barth, *Church Dogmatics,* 4 vols., ed. Thomas F. Torrance, trans. Geoffrey W. Bromiley (Edinburgh: T. & T. Clark, 1936-1969), I/2: 362-454.

24. Barth, *Church Dogmatics,* I/2: 400.

25. Barth, *Church Dogmatics,* I/2: 453.

26. Barth, *Church Dogmatics,* I/2: 453.

27. Barth, *Church Dogmatics,* I/2: 401.

neighbor. And just as we love God in being thankful, so we love the neighbor in bearing witness to what God has done in Jesus Christ. Barth does not mean by this merely a subjective feeling, but an inclination of the heart worked out in corporate worship, the bearing of a Christian witness, and acts of justice and mercy. This witness is confession that the Word which we have heard in the preaching of the church is true. "It is basically an expository word, the explaining and applying of Holy Scripture as the primal witness to Jesus Christ which underlies and sustains all the rest. It is when I speak a word like this to my neighbour that I fulfil my responsibility to him."[28] Here we have a statement of a covenantal understanding of Christian doxology.

It is the covenantal understanding of worship that has been largely responsible in the last few decades for a revival of church architecture in both Roman Catholic and Protestant circles. This is particularly evident in such places as the Netherlands, Switzerland, and the German Rhineland, where a covenantal understanding of worship has traditionally played an important role. The best architects of our century have been called upon to rethink the nature of the space in which Christian worship is to be celebrated. Discussing the matter with pastors and theologians, these architects have built a number of surprisingly beautiful churches. Although the style of architecture has invariably been that of the twentieth century, the thinking behind the style is inspired by classical principles of Christian worship.

Both in Europe and in this country there has been a conscious departure from the neo-Gothic approach to building churches.[29]

---

28. Barth, *Church Dogmatics,* I/2: 443.
29. Among the more important challenges to neo-Gothic churches is the work of two contemporary American theologians, James Hastings Nichols and Leonard Trinterude; see their report *The Architectural Setting for Reformed Worship* (Chicago: Presbytery of Chicago, 1960).

The neo-Gothic movement, largely fostered by the Romanticism of the last century, was led by the "High Church" movement, which originated in England but quickly spread to America. A somewhat similar movement in Germany was led by Wilhelm Löhe. The "High Church" movement wanted to reassert the centrality of the eucharist and deemphasize the preaching of the Word. It was concerned with cultivating the distinction between "clergy" and "laity." While the choir, robed to look like medieval monks, was to enrich the service by singing introits, anthems, and responses, the singing of the congregation was regarded as of minor significance. The liturgical goal of the "High Church" movement was to give a mystical feeling to worship. Beclouding the whole thing in mystery was looked upon very favorably. The movement endorsed a return to medieval architecture and the medieval liturgical calendar as ways of erasing the effects of both the Protestant Reformation and, incidentally, the American Revolution. "High Churchmen" were Tories through and through.

The recent renaissance of church architecture was in part a reaction against the "High Church" emphases, but it was also a conscious departure from the architectural forms of revivalism. By the middle of the nineteenth century, in their concern to be "nondenominational," the prominent evangelists of the period had driven a wedge between the sacraments and evangelism. Both the Sunday School movement and the revival movement had prospered under the leadership of such men as Dwight L. Moody and Billy Sunday who found it greatly to their advantage that they had neither theological education nor ministerial ordination. There was a strong inclination to avoid a "churchy" feeling in their meetings on the grounds that it would make the prospective converts uncomfortable. Choirs and soloists began to function as sacred entertainment to help draw a crowd of "unreached" people to whom the gospel could be presented. These movements had their effect on church architecture. By the end of the last century the typical Protestant church was dominated by a speaker's platform, behind which was ranged a choir loft and towering rows of organ pipes. Neither communion table nor baptismal font was of any visual importance. There were usually large balconies and several adjacent rooms that could be opened up for Sunday School conventions and evangelistic rallies. Clearly, the assembling together of the faithful for formal worship was not the most important function of the building. The old Akron Plan churches of several generations ago expressed the opposite extreme from the neo-Gothic churches of the same period.

The art of architecture is to construct buildings that serve their intended functions in such a way that they are beautiful. Beauty is the primary concern of art. Architecture is a special kind of art in which the beauty arises from function. One might express its uniqueness by saying that architecture is a piece of art in which we live. The beauty of craftsmanship is accentuated in architecture. A great architect must have the service of master craftsmen. He must have a sense of what kind of life is supposed to be lived in the building he is to design as well as a sense of how stone, concrete, wood, steel, and glass are to be used beautifully. He must have an appreciation of great craftsmanship in the use of the materials. This is the striking thing about so many of these churches. What has happened is that a number of architects have begun to help us build our churches so that they really do serve the purpose for which the church comes together. A good architect can help us see the beauty of limestone walls, oaken timbers, and even steel girders, but a good architect can also show us the beauty of an assembly of people gathered together.

A worshiping assembly is very different from a theater crowd or a lecture audience. A worshiping assembly interacts. We sing praises together, and of the very essence of that act of worship is the way the singing of others lifts us up to join in the song. We gather around the Lord's Table one with

133

another to share the loaf and the cup. That we are both served by our neighbor and serve our neighbor is of the essence of the sacrament. This at least would be the way covenantal doxology would approach it. The same is true with baptism. Of the nature of the sacrament is receiving it in the midst of the people of God. Again, one would need to make a similar point with preaching. Christian preaching is a community activity. Real preaching begins to take place when the preacher can read some sort of reaction in the faces of the congregation. Outstanding oratory cannot come from reading a text word-for-word as it has been written out beforehand in the study. Preaching is like tennis: it has to respond to those sitting in the pew. And for this to happen, the congregation has to be close enough to the minister so that he can see how the members of the congregation are returning his serves. An alive congregation makes for lively preaching. A well-designed building can help enormously in bringing this about. This, too, has to do with the art of architecture.

Particularly in Switzerland, Germany, and the Netherlands, church architects since the Second World War have made significant progress in housing the worship assembly in spaces that promote Christian worship. The city of Zurich has several particularly fine churches. One thinks of the Bullinger Church and the Alstetten Church, just to begin the list. The Bethlehem Church in Bern is another fine building where the congregation is gathered around three sides of a very simple yet prominent table and pulpit. In the Netherlands one thinks of the Maranatha Church in Amsterdam and the Reformed Church in the town of Aerdenhout.[30] The Netherlands is filled with beautiful examples of contemporary architecture. It is not surprising that the same sense of style and good taste is to be found in its churches.

30. For pictures of these and other contemporary European churches, see Donald J. Bruggink and Carl H. Droppers, *Christ and Architecture* (Grand Rapids: William B. Eerdmans, 1965).

Several features of these churches are particularly worthy of notice. First and most important, the architecture of these churches supports a covenantal understanding of worship in that it emphasizes the covenantal bond that unites in one body all the members of the church in the ministry of praise and prayer, the ministry of the Word, and the sacraments of baptism and the Lord's Supper. This is true whether the members function in the main body of the worshiping assembly or as musicians, as ministers of the sacrament, as preachers of the Word, as elders, or as deacons. This does not mean that some sort of egalitarian spirit has tried to ignore the special calling or charisma of certain members of the congregation. The role of the pastor and elders in presiding over the congregation is often specifically recognized by the placement of their seating, and yet they are definitely part of the assembly. The importance of the reading and preaching of the Scriptures is usually recognized by a prominent pulpit on which rests an open Bible. One thing almost always found in these new churches is that the communion table is given a much greater importance than it was in Protestant churches of the last century. There is a conscious attempt to achieve a balance between pulpit and table. In one way or another it is shown that the whole congregation assembles around the table, in distinction to the way so many neo-Gothic churches suggest that the "altar" is ministered to exclusively by the "clergy." In much the same way, an attempt is almost always made to show that the choir is part of the congregation rather than a group of performers giving a show before an audience. The covenantal nature of baptism is likewise expressed by placing the font so that the sacrament is celebrated in the midst of the assembled congregation on the Lord's Day rather than in a special chapel at the door of the church and then only on Saturday morning or Sunday afternoon.

Another feature one often finds is that the pulpit, the table, and the choir loft are arranged in a dynamic relation to each

135

other so that it is clear that all are essential to the celebration of Christian worship. Several years ago I remember worshiping for a number of weeks in a church in one of the suburbs of Zurich. The church was small, but it was built with superb craftsmanship. The thing I remember most about it was that the church was filled with light. The whole service of worship had a marvelous vitality. The table with the communion silver upon it stood toward the center of the room. This arrangement itself became a symbol. Whether the sacrament was celebrated on that particular Sunday or not, worship was always celebrated around the table. The congregation was gathered around its three sides. There were chairs for the elders on both sides of the table and a chair for the pastor behind it. I particularly noticed that prayers were offered from behind the table, while the pulpit was reserved for the reading and preaching of the Scriptures. Having a large Bible open on the pulpit emphasized its symbolic function. The pulpit was against the east wall, but projected fairly well out into the room, so that one had the feeling that the congregation was gathered around the pulpit too. The choir loft with its organ was on the west wall. The two seemed to balance each other, the pulpit on the east wall and choir loft on the west wall facing each other. It was done in such a way that the organ with its ranks of exposed pipes was a symbol of the ministry of praise, just as the pulpit with its open Bible was a symbol of the ministry of the Word. The whole experience was one of assembling together in the presence of God to serve God in worship, and the building was so skillfully designed that it promoted exactly that. The builders had done their job with care and skill, and consequently it was beautiful.

Covenant theology offers us a means of understanding the relationship of many different dimensions of Christian worship. It suggests to us the balance between Word and sacrament, between the service of God and the service of the neighbor. It helps us understand the importance of assembling together and offers us a means of integrating the ministry of evangelism and the ministry of praise and thanksgiving. Covenantal theology helps us travel the road from epiclesis to eucharist. And this is of the essence of the Christian life, this movement from crying out to God in our need to blessing God for our salvation.

# Index of Scripture References

| Luke | | 11:25 | 11, 118 |
|---|---|---|---|
| 2:11 | 51 | 12–14 | 118 |
| 2:14 | 51 | 13 | 120 |
| 4:18-19 | 48-49 | 13:1 | 7 |
| 19:41 | 109 | 14:26 | 118 |
| 24:28-33 | 105 | 15:1-2 | 49 |

| John | 63 | Galatians | |
|---|---|---|---|
| 1:1 | 66, 72, 80, 82 | 4:6 | 32 |
| 1:4-5 | 66, 72, 80, 82 | | |
| 1:14 | 66, 72, 80, 82 | Ephesians | |
| 2:1-11 | 67, 68, 74 | 5:19 | 97 |
| 4:23-24 | 3, 9, 95, 96 | | |
| 6:4 | 12 | Colossians | 100 |
| 6:35-40 | 80 | 3:16 | 97 |
| 6:48 | 81 | | |
| 6:51 | 81 | 1 Timothy | |
| 14–17 | 25 | 2:1-8 | 25 |
| 14:13 | 25 | | |
| 15:16 | 25 | Hebrews | |
| 16:23-24 | 25 | 12:28 | 96 |
| 20:29 | 67 | 13:15 | 71 |
| 20:31 | 67 | | |
| | | James | 63 |
| Acts | 9 | 5:17-18 | 11 |
| 6:4 | 25 | | |
| 17:29 | 97 | 1 Peter | |
| | | 2:4-9 | 26 |
| | | 2:4-10 | 11 |
| Romans | | 2:5 | 96 |
| 5:8 | 125 | 2:9 | 49 |
| 12:1 | 96, 97 | | |
| | | 1 John | |
| 1 Corinthians | | 1:1 | 80 |
| 10–14 | 9 | | |
| 10:1-13 | 11 | Revelation | 12, 50 |
| 10:16 | 117 | 5:12 | 49 |
| 10:21 | 117 | 19:6 | 50 |
| 11:18 | 117 | 19:9 | 67, 68, 74-75, 86 |

# Index of Subjects and Names